"As a layman and Sunday school teacher I lean heavily on gifted teachers, that not only go by The Book, but communicate God's truth in an encouraging and "user friendly" way. Having been in the Baptist Church my entire life, I've become weary of the variety of new "Programs" presented to the congregation in attempts to encourage more participation and more professions of faith. Most fizzle out in just a few months.

Ken and Mike's work captures the heart, mission, and enthusiasm of the Church as described in Acts closer than anything I've ever studied. Having the privilege of knowing him personally, I see a man whose life and work give a testimony of the Abundant Daily Life available to anyone committed to introducing others to Jesus."

— Scott Coleman
Sunday School teacher, Kirbywood Baptist Church, Germantown, TN

"Reaching people is hard work. Churches exert much blood, sweat, and tears to reach those in their communities. But often, we lose sight of making sure those we work so hard to reach get connected. We labor diligently on the front door of the church while the back door is swung wide open. Enter *V.E.L.C.R.O. Church*. Mike James and Dr. Hemphill have done an outstanding job showing us how we can keep those we are reaching. This study will be an invaluable resource for every church."

— Allan Taylor
Minister of Education, First Baptist Church, Woodstock, GA

V.E.L.C.R.O. CHURCH

V.E.L.C.R.O. CHURCH

KEN HEMPHILL
MIKE JAMES

Auxano
PRESS
Tigerville, South Carolina
www.AuxanoPress.com

Dedicated to the members of

Wolf Creek Baptist
First Baptist Galax
First Baptist Norfolk

These wonderful people embraced and
employed revitalization principles that
produced healthy kingdom expansion.

-Ken Hemphill

This book is dedicated to two special people in my life:

To my beautiful wife and best friend, Kathy
for being such an important partner with me in ministry.
The Lord smiled on me when he brought us together
to experience this life journey.
You are the best!

To Michael, my son who carries
not only my name but my heart, I am so proud of you.
Your smile brightens my day and I thank our Heavenly Father
that He allowed me the joy to be your Dad.

I am truly blessed by both of you.
-Mike James

Contents

Preface   xi

Acknowledgements   xix

Valuing Every Person as a Gift of God   1

Engaging Every Guest with Intentionality   15

Leading Our Friends to Christ   35

Connecting to Community   47

Recognizing Relationships as the Key to Assimilation   61

Organizing Small Groups for Ongoing Care   75

Preface

If you are an outdoorsman at all, I'm sure you have been frustrated by the burrs that often attach themselves to your socks. Not only are they annoying and sometimes painful, they also can be nearly impossible to remove from your clothing. Next time you find yourself agitated by such an inconvenience, think of Velcro.

Swiss electrical engineer George de Mestral was enjoying a hunting trip with his dog in the Alps when he encountered those annoying burrs we all love to hate. As he took a close look at the seeds of burdock that kept sticking to his clothes and the dog's fur, he began to see the potential for a new kind of fastener. He examined the burrs under a microscope and noticed hundreds of hooks that caught on anything with a loop such as clothing or animal fur. You guessed it—Velcro was conceived.

As you might imagine, most people refused to take seriously his idea for a new kind of fastener. He took his invention to Lyon, which was then the center of weaving. One weaver helped him by making two cotton strips that worked but wore out so quickly that they were not viable. Undeterred, George settled on nylon, a new invention. It had several advantages. It did not rot, break down, or attract mold, and could be produced in threads of varying thicknesses.

George discovered that when nylon was sewn under hot infrared light, it forms nearly perfect hooks for the hook side of the fastener. He still had to discover a way to make the loops that would connect with the hooks. On the verge of giving up, he bought a pair of shears and trimmed the tops off the loops, thus creating hooks that would match up perfectly with the loops in the pile. Mechanizing the process took eight years and an additional year to create the loom that trimmed the loops after weaving them. In all, it took ten years to create a Velcro production that worked. There is something to say for tenacity.

The commercial acceptance of Velcro as a "zipperless zipper" was slow in coming. Velcro got its first break when the aerospace industry used it to help astronauts to maneuver in and out of bulky space suits. Skiers saw the similarities between their costumes and those of astronauts and introduced Velcro to the ski business. After seeing astronauts store food in pouches on the walls and stand upright in a weightless atmosphere, children's clothing makers came onboard. And the rest is history.

Velcro is the brand name of the first commercially marketed fabric hook-and-loop fastener. George invented it 1941 and patented it in 1955, finally bringing it to commercial use in the late 1950s. The word "Velcro" combines two French words *velours* and *crochet* or hook.

Velcro consists of two components, the first of which features tiny hooks and the second features even smaller "hairier" loops. When the two faces are pressed together, the hooks catch in the loops and the two pieces fasten themselves together. Velcro fasteners made from Teflon loops, polyester hooks, and glass backing are used in aerospace applications.

The Velcro brand is a good example of a genericized trademark—a brand name that has become the generic term for a type of product. Besides being used as a generic term for hook and loop fasteners, the word "Velcro" has now become a verb. To be "Velcroed" means to be attached by Velcro.[1]

Applying Velcro to the Church

Wouldn't it be wonderful if we could attach one side of Velcro to our church and the other to everyone who visits so that they would become permanently stuck to the body of Christ? Tragically many churches more often resemble Teflon rather than Velcro. People come for a visit and then they simply don't return. In other cases they actually enroll in a small group or even join the church, but then in time they just seem to "slip away."

Here are the facts that help explain why we desperately need to "Velcroize" our churches.

FOUR VELCRO FACTS

FACT #1:   Your church cannot grow without guests.

FACT #2:   Your church cannot grow if your guests don't come back!

FACT #3:   You never get a second chance to make a great first impression.

FACT #4:   Your church cannot grow if people join, and then drop out!

FACT #1 is an obvious truth. Churches need a steady flow of guests coming through the front door in order to experience healthy growth. One reason for this is because the church's back door is often left open. Most churches lose 6-10% of their people each year because of attrition, death, transfer or simple apathy.[2] We can't do much about the death rate or people who are transferred because of their job, but we can do so much more to keep the ones we have from walking out the back door. Reaching and keeping people is not only biblical in fulfilling the Great Commission, but it is also the only practical means of keeping a church vibrant and alive.

As we will discover in our study, getting guests to attend is simply the first step. The second step is getting them to stick and stay. Healthy churches should average five percent of their average worship attendance each Sunday as guests.[3] In other words, if your attendance is 200, you should have approximately 10 guests each week to remain healthy. Your church could have the best student and children's program in town, the finest facilities, and the most dynamic preacher in your state, but if you don't have a steady stream of new guests each week, your church will plateau and eventually decline because of the natural attrition rate.

But having guests does not translate into healthy kingdom growth unless those guests are retained. Charles Arn reports that the average non-growing church has a visitor retention rate of 10-12%, which means that ten to twelve guests out of 100 are involved in the church one year after their first visit. Growing churches, on the other hand, average 25% percent retention rate![4] Growing churches will manage to Velcro twice as many guests to their church as the non-growing church. The purpose of this book is to help your church raise the retention rate in order to reach and Velcro more of your guests and members into the life of your church.

Here's a simple question worth your consideration. In the course of a year, how many people do you have to reach in order to have a net gain of one person? Your net growth is figured by taking the number of new members for the year and then subtracting the members who move away, join another church, drop out, or die.

In one church I consulted we conducted a five-year study of membership growth. The church experienced 541 additions by letter or baptism during this five-year period. On the surface this would appear to be very healthy growth, but the plateaued attendance indicated that something else was happening beneath the surface. When deletions by transfers and deaths were factored into the equation, we discovered that over this same five-year period the church lost 535 members. The net gain was only six people over five years! Based on these averages, this particular church must reach a minimum of 107 new persons each year just to maintain the present attendance level. This church will not experience any net growth statistically unless they reach more than 108 people per year. This church like many others had lost its Velcro!

Bottom Line: If your back door is open as wide as your front door, you will not experience healthy growth.

Yes, "Houston we have a problem!" We have no desire to waste any more ink on describing the problem. We already know that a large majority of churches are plateaued because they fail to attract and keep newcomers. We want this book to be encouraging and to provide numerous ideas that you can employ in your community and in your church to solve the Teflon problem so that your church can be known as a Velcro church.

A Simple Overview

We have used the acrostic **V.E.L.C.R.O.** to outline the process to aid in retention and application. Each chapter includes a Bible study to be used in a small group setting and ideas that can be employed both personally and corporately. Each chapter includes several different ideas so that you can select those which best fit your church in its unique setting. This is no "cookie cutter" book that gives you a new program of assimilation. It is a book that will allow you to plan a process that will work in your community and in your church.

The first chapter, "**V**aluing Every Person as a Gift from God" is the first step in the Velcro process and occurs before any guest visits your church. We have been guilty of treating the church as the "Field of Dreams." We assume that "if we build it they will come." This has never been the case, nor is it the case today. Different researchers have shown that somewhere between 79% to 86% of people are members of the church they now attend because they were brought by a friend or relative. We give you practical, natural, and fun ideas to encourage you to encounter people in the marketplace and build a relationship that will enable you to bring them to your church and to Christ.

The second chapter, "Engaging Every Guest With Intentionality" takes us to the moment your friend first comes in contact with your small group or church family and follows them until they are attached. Once again Bible study is followed by numerous practical suggestions. The key word is "intentional." Most churches fail at this step because they are not intentional.

The third chapter is "Leading Friends to Christ." We provide simple ways of showing how the church family can join together to introduce people to Christ. Once people are involved in a small group and exposed to the teaching of God's Word, they are well on their way to making a meaningful and life-changing commitment to Christ. After all, our goal is kingdom expansion through conversion, not simply numerical church growth.

The fourth chapter entitled, "Connecting New Family Members to Community," shows you how to connect people to the church family and small groups in such a way that they are integrally involved in the activities of the church. This will involve new members' orientation strategy that actually works. It will also help you to improve the "stickiness" of your small groups.

The fifth chapter, "Recognizing Relationships as the Key" moves us a step further in the Velcro process. Studies indicate that when people become involved in ministry they remain connected to community. We show you how to help people discover their unique giftedness and thus find a meaningful place of service in the body. When people feel needed, they will be stuck to community.

The final chapter, "Organizing Small Groups for Continual Care," provides you with a process to ensure that family needs are met with consistency and regularity. We want you to consider the ISSE formula—Intentional, Sustainable, Simple and Expandable. The care group ministry organized through the small groups best fits these four criteria and is explained in detail.

We promise that this book will challenge you from God's Word and inspire you to find meaningful application in your church. The ideas presented here will work in any size church in any setting. If you allow God to change your heart and guide your thinking by His Word, you will be able to create a Velcro community. We are indebted to many writers who have tackled this subject including the book, *Truth That Sticks; How to Communicate Velcro Truth in a Teflon World*, by Avery Willis Jr. and Mark Snowden, Navpress, 2010 which is an excellent book on the methodology of making disciples.

All additional helps needed to promote and teach this material are provided free online from Auxanopress.com. There are indicated in the book with the letters ROL (resources on line).

---

1   Information about Velcro from Wickipedia.

2   Win and Charles Arn, *The Church Growth Ratio Book* (Monrovia, CA.: Church Growth Inc. 2004), p.48.

3   Ibid p.47

4   Ibid p.50

Acknowledgements

The idea from this book came from my good friend, Mike James, who is my co-author for the book. Mike served on staff with me in Norfolk, Virginia and now works for the Kentucky Baptist Convention. The idea for the acrostic V.E.L.C.R.O. for teaching assimilation in the book came from a lecture he did for me at Southern Seminary.

We are praying that this book will be a catalyst that God uses to help your small group or church think strategically about reaching and keeping people through the local church. The format of the book is totally new. It is designed and written for small group study. Each chapter begins with Bible study and the church assimilation strategy flows naturally from the Biblical text. It is our conviction that nothing changes hearts and minds but the word of God applied by the Spirit of God.

Both Mike and I are indebted to our wives, Paula Hemphill and Kathy James, partners in ministry who give us both the freedom and encouragement to travel, speak, and write. Our families are the context of our ministry.

It is an honor to publish with Auxano Press whose ministry statement is to provide biblically sound tools to help individuals and their churches to experience balanced growth. The folks at Auxano Press are a delight to work with. I want to thank my good friend Joe McKeever for the cover artwork.

For the sake of simplicity and brevity, Mike and I have used footnotes sparingly. We have both profited by the reading of numerous books on the topic of assimilation.

Free small group study guides for *V.E.L.C.R.O. Church* are available from AuxanoPress.com.

This book is one of a growing number of biblical resources to encourage church health from The Center for Church Planting and Revitalization at North Greenville University. I would like to thank President Jimmy Epting and my colleagues at NGU for all their help and encouragement as we seek together to revitalize local churches.

Ken Hemphill
Travelers Rest, South Carolina
Fall 2011

CHAPTER ONE

Valuing Every Person as a Gift of God

How do you view daily interruptions? You know what I mean. You have a large "to-do-list," and in the grocery store, you run into a neighbor you haven't seen for a while. Or maybe you are running a little late for an important event and an old friend you have been praying for just seems to show up in your path? Do you see such events as divine interruptions and wonderful opportunities for showing someone love and sharing Christ, or do you see them as an unwelcome intrusion into your already over-crowded calendar? How did Jesus respond when the woman with the issue of blood grabbed His cloak while He was on the way to heal the daughter of Jairus, or when He was approached by unclean lepers? When we read the Gospels, it appears that much of Jesus' day was totally unscripted. Upon closer examination, we discover that Jesus treats each "unscripted" moment as a gift from the Father.

Let's try another approach to the same question. How do you respond when you encounter that neighbor who has been a thorn in the flesh? Do you find yourself trying to avoid the people in your community who aren't very loveable? How about those folks whose lifestyle is contrary to everything you believe? How did Jesus respond when He encountered a woman who was living in adultery and had already dispatched five husbands? How did He respond to a tax collector who had taken advantage of his position for personal gain?

What compelled Jesus to value every person as a gift of God and to see each interruption as a kingdom moment? Let's learn from the Master Himself. You may recall that Jesus' "rather unusual" behavior often caused members of the religious establishment of His day (Pharisees and scribes) to complain that He spent too much time with sinners.

Could our problem be that we spend too little time with sinners to be effective in reaching them with the Good News? When was the last occasion you intentionally spent time with a lost friend with the goal of building a bridge for sharing the incredible good news that God loves them so much He sent Jesus to die for them? Perhaps you have been intimidated or even "turned-off" by the thought of evangelism. You don't feel gifted to share, or you think evangelism is pushy and presumptive. Don't quit reading, I think you will like the Velcro approach which is taken from the life and teaching of Jesus.

Let's take a moment to sit at the Master's feet. We will study Luke 15. This passage will help us to understand the motivation behind the sacrificial lifestyle of Jesus that compelled Him to give up heavenly glory to come to earth to save sinners like us. Jesus accomplished more than anyone in history and yet He never seemed rushed. He simply ministered as He was on the way. Learning from the Master will help us to reach friends naturally without feeling that we have to add "something else" to our schedule.

It will be helpful for you to have your Bible open as you study through this book. Feel free to mark important verses in your Bible and write notes in the spaces provided in this book.

Putting the text in its context.
If you take a moment to look back at Luke 14 you will find a story about Jesus sharing a meal with one of the Pharisees on the Sabbath. It is noteworthy that Jesus was a friend of all sinners, including those in the "religious establishment."

One particular phrase in verse one of chapter fourteen suggest that this invitation to lunch came from less than pure motives on the part of the Pharisees—"they were watching Him closely." The Pharisees were always attempting to create a situation where they could accuse Jesus of blasphemy or at least diminish His popularity. In this case, the Pharisees had arranged to have a man suffering from dropsy placed in front of Jesus. We can tell this is a trap since the Pharisees would usually avoid contact with the sick, believing that their illness was the result of personal sin. They knew that Jesus' compassionate character would compel Him to minister to the helpless man and thus break traditional Sabbath restrictions.

Jesus understands and unmasks their motives by asking several questions. He first asks whether it is lawful to heal on the Sabbath (v. 3). They refuse to answer and Jesus heals the man. He then asks which of them would not come to the rescue of a son or even an ox that fell into a well on the Sabbath (v. 5). Once again they are unable to respond. They have been caught in their own trap. Why would someone treat an animal better than they would a needy person?

Jesus seizes the moment to teach them several kingdom principles through parables. A parable is an earthly story with a heavenly message. Noticing at lunch that the men were choosing places of honor for themselves, He indicates that when invited to a wedding feast one should humbly choose the last place and allow the host to move them to a higher place if he so desires (14:7-11). Jesus goes to the heart of Pharisaic sin— pride. Do we ever allow an inflated notion of our spiritual importance to cause us to look down on those we consider unrighteous and undeserving?

Jesus then addresses His host telling him that when giving a dinner party a man should not simply invite friends and relatives who will therefore invite him in return. If one's only motive in giving the party is to curry the favor of friends, that will be their only reward for their effort. Jesus suggests that they should have used the party as an event that would have allowed them to invite the poor, the crippled, the lame, and the blind (14:12-14). These categories represent those people in Jesus' day who were viewed as the outcasts of society, the unrighteous. This text requires us to answer another difficult question. How long has it been since any one of us has invited a lost friend to our home, church, or small group?

Jesus was speaking to the religious pride that kept the Pharisees from coming to Him for the forgiveness of their sin. Don't miss the fact that Jesus wanted the Pharisees to respond to His offer of forgiveness as much as He wanted any other sinner to respond. Do we sometimes allow our spiritual pride to keep us from associating with sinners who need Christ? Have we forgotten that we were all sinners before we met Christ and experienced His grace?

Jesus tells a third and final parable (14:16-23). A man had planned a big dinner party and had sent out invitations. As the time of the event arrives, he sends a servant to tell them all the preparations for the big event had been made. Each of the invited guests makes excuses for their lack of interest. The head of the household instructs his servant to—"Go out at once into the streets and lanes of the city and bring in here the poor and crippled and blind and lame" (14:21). The servant indicates that there is still room in the banquet hall and the master says, "Go out into the highways and the hedges, and compel them to come in, so that my house may be filled" (14:23). Did you notice that when room remains the search is broadened and the compulsion becomes more intense?

Are you ever too narrow in your search? Are you too easily discouraged when someone makes an excuse? How can we compel people to come to the feast prepared by Jesus without being pushy?

The scene changes as Jesus continues His ministry journey. Large crowds are now following Jesus, some out of curiosity and self-interest, but others out of personal need. Jesus speaks of what is demanded if one desires to become a disciple (14:25-35). He indicates that the person must be willing to put Christ above all earthly desires and attachments. Discipleship demands that one first count the costs of following Jesus. When one makes a commitment to Christ he/she promises the world a truly transformed life (salt) but, if it is a shallow commitment, it delivers an insipid (tasteless) life which has no value in presenting Christ to the world.

Before we look at our passage which explains why Jesus spent so much time with sinners, each one of us must ask whether my life is truly salty. Do I present convincing evidence that Christ has transformed my life? Christian witness involves both demonstration and presentation. Before we can compel the needy to come to the party provided by Jesus, we must be sure that we have counted the cost and are fully-committed followers of Christ.

Encountering the Word

Verse one of Luke chapter 15 indicates that those aware of their own spiritual needs were drawn to Jesus like metal filings to a magnet. They were drawn because they sensed that He loved them unconditionally. It was Jesus' friendship with sinners that caused the Pharisees and scribes to grumble, saying, "This man receives sinners and eats with them" (15:2). Jesus' response to this accusation is found in the three parables that follow.

5

These three parables are told in a sequence. All three are important for our understanding of the focus of Jesus ministry and the passion of His life. All three parables share certain similarities. In each parable there is something that is missing and each concludes with an earthly celebration that mirrors the heavenly party that occurs each time one sinner repents.

The first story (15:4-7) concerns a man who has a hundred sheep, a relatively small flock. A little background information about the life and work of shepherds in the time of Jesus may prove helpful. This was a time of the open range and therefore the shepherd would rise early in the morning to lead his sheep to open pasture. As the season wore on and good pasture became more difficult to find, the shepherd would be required to travel further and further from home to provide for his sheep. For that reason, the shepherd would often spend the night in the open range with his sheep. To protect his sheep in the evening, he would drive them into a sheltered place and lay his body across the entrance, keeping his sheep in and any wild animal out (cf. John 10:1-18).

One evening as the shepherd is counting his sheep in preparation for the night's rest, he discovers one is missing. I have always imagined that the missing sheep is the "proverbial black sheep" who seems to be the one who always challenges our patience. Once the shepherd discovers that a single sheep is missing, he leaves the ninety-nine and goes after the one which is lost, searching "until he finds it." When he comes back with his lost sheep, he calls together his friends and neighbors so they can celebrate the return of the one that was lost.

Here are four principles we should underline about the search of the shepherd. 1) He searched because he understood the condition of a lost sheep. 2) He was pro-active and immediate in his search. 3) He was intentional. 4) He was determined. He was prepared to search "until he found" the sheep.

The second parable is about a woman who loses one of ten coins. The mention of the woman without reference to a husband leads us to think she is a widow. It is likely that the ten silver coins was all that stood between this woman and starvation. This was her social security allotment; her SEP IRA. Once again we see the immediacy of the search as she lights a lamp and begins to search before the light of day. We also notice the theme of thoroughness as she sweeps her house with the determination to "search carefully until she finds it" (15:8).

The final parable is told in much greater detail. It provides the culmination and focal point for Jesus' teaching. We often refer to this parable as the parable of "the prodigal son." The story is straightforward and moving. It begins with a simple declaration—"A man had two sons" (15:11). The failure to mention a wife may indicate that the two boys are all who remain of this man's family. The younger son comes to the father and asks that he be given the portion of the estate that would fall to him. It is worthy of note that under Jewish law the younger boy would not inherit the estate and thus would end up working for his older brother. It may have been this reality and the obvious sibling rivalry that prompted the boy to seek his inheritance while his father remained alive.

The father does not hesitate and the younger son departs for a "distant country" where he promptly squandered his entire estate through sinful dissipation. At this point he encounters the "perfect storm"—he is out of money, out of friends, and without a job. We can be sure he has sunk to the depths when we read that he was willing to feed swine for a living. He didn't just become a swine-herder, he was glad to eat with the swine (15:16). Sin will always take one further than he intends to go and cause him to sink deeper than he ever imagined possible.

At the depth of his despair, he begins to think of home. He realizes that his father's hired servants had plenty to eat while he was starving. He determines to swallow his pride, confess his sin, and return home as a servant. He couldn't imagine that he would ever deserve to be treated as a son again. While he was still at a distance from his home, his father met him with kisses and a warm embrace. There is a phrase in verse 20 that we must not miss—"his father saw him and felt compassion for him."

The embraces and kisses are followed by gifts as the father instructs the servants to bring out the best robe, a ring, and sandals for his feet. The ring is the most important gift. It tells us both of the depth of depravity of man's sin and the height of mercy of the Father's love. The ring was likely a "signet" ring engraved with a family crest, allowing one to sign a contract as a member of the family. The signet ring would be impressed into hot wax, sealing the document and ratifying a contract. In sin, the son had willingly placed his father's estate at risk. In grace, the father restored the prodigal to sonship.

Like the first two parables, this one ends with a party. The father demands that the fatted calf be killed "for this son of mine was dead and has come to life again; he was lost and has been found" (15:24). But this parable ends with a twist. The elder brother refuses to join the party. He hears the sounds of a party while he is still at work in the field. When he asks a servant about the merriment, he is told that his brother has been received back safe and sound.

If you expected him to join the celebration, you will be disappointed. He became angry and was unwilling to go in to the party. His compassionate father pleads with him to join the party. He responds with obvious hostility, claiming that his father had treated him unfairly. He points to his years of service and his obedience to each and every command without any reward from the father. Listen to this angry accusation—"…when this son of yours came, who has devoured your wealth with prostitutes, you killed the fatted calf for him" (15:30). The father answers—"Son, you have always been with me, and all that is mine is yours. But we had to celebrate and rejoice, for this brother of yours was dead and has begun to live, and was lost and has been found" (15:31-32).

Did you notice the progression in the three stories? First there was one of a hundred sheep missing and then one in ten coins and finally one in two sons. Further we move from sheep to silver to human life—a son's life. There is both increasing scarcity and increasing value. Now, here's a trick question. I mentioned that in all three parables there is a missing item. First a missing sheep followed by a missing coin. What is the missing component in the final parable? Here's a clue—it is not the prodigal. It is the "rescuer!" No one looked for the missing boy.

Applying the Word

1. Why was the shepherd willing to leave the 99 sheep and look for the one?

He understood the condition of the lost sheep

2. Write the phrase that indicates how long the shepherd was prepared to look for the lost sheep.

as long as it takes to find the sheep

3. What would have become of the sheep if the shepherd had not found him?

He would have been killed by wild animals

4. Did it occur to you that the shepherd was risking his life by looking for the sheep. What do you risk, when you go after a lost friend?

began rejection

5. Why did the woman refuse to wait until morning?

the coins were all she had

6. What was the unique point of the first two parables?

something was lost and someone went to search for it until it was found

7. With so much at stake, why did no one look for the younger brother?

sibling rivalry and it was the desire of the young man to not work for his brother

8. What are your feelings about why the prodigal left home?

It was a bad decision

9. Why do you think sinners remain alienated from God?

they do not want to give up the life still they are living

10. What was the greatest barrier that kept the young man from returning home?

pride

11. What most surprises you about the Father?

He did not ask him any question but accepted him back unconditionly

12. Why do you think the elder brother never went to look for his lost brother?

He was unconsired about the wellfaire of his brother

13. Do you think it would have been easier for the young man to return home, if his brother had come looking for him with news of his father's compassion for him?

yes

14. Who does the elder brother represent in this story and why?

A person who will not help others who are lost   Jews

15. Do we sometimes behave like the older brother?

yes

How?

Here is a truth that the Lord has taught me as I have considered this parable. The elder brother knew that the father would restore the prodigal to sonship if he returned. The elder brother hated the actions of his younger brother who had wasted his father's estate and thus did not want him to return. When your love for your brother does not motivate you to look for your prodigal, your love for your Father must move you to action.

Make it Stick

Personal Actions

- List three prodigals who you want to see return/come to the Father. Your list should contain the names of "pre-Christians" and persons who have been saved but have strayed from the Father's home.

- Commit to pray that God would convict these prodigals of their sin and create the desire to come to the Father.

- Ask the Father to allow you to lead the search for a prodigal for whom you have been praying.

- Look for daily opportunities to show God's love to people you casually meet in the course of the day. Effective "valuing" must become a life-style 24/7. As you go through your normal daily activities, ask the Father to show you His activity. You can approach every person you encounter each day with the confidence that God is at work in his/her life. Ask questions that show you care about them as persons; ask them how you can pray for them.

- Plan one loving action that you can take over the next several weeks that will assist the prodigal to undertake the return trip. This loving action can be as simple as a drop-in visit with cookies, a handwritten note or meeting for a cup of coffee. Spontaneous loving actions are the water that helps the seed of the gospel come to life.

- As you build relationships with colleagues and neighbors, invite them to be your guest in your small group. Did you know that about 8 out of 10 persons attend their present church because they were invited by a friend or relative?

Group Actions

- Ask members, who are willing to share names of prodigals they are praying for and create a small group prodigal prayer list.

- Organize your small group into prayer triplets. You can meet together weekly or pray over the phone. Each person should share the names you listed above as "prodigals." Your "prodigal" list should include persons who are pre-Christian and persons who have been saved but strayed from the Father's home. Each prayer partner will pray in turn for every person listed. Each prayer triplet will be praying for nine persons. Ask the Lord to prepare the heart of the individual and give you an opportunity to be the person who aids them as they return to the Father.

- Plan regular events through your small group for people who are not presently involved in any church or small group Bible study. For example, you might plan a fellowship gathering at someone's house or a local park to make friends feel comfortable. This is a "sowing" event. The focus should be on fun and fellowship.

- Plan a "friend day" in your small group where each person is encouraged to bring a friend. The emphasis is on "bring" not just invite. Each person can bring a dish and have brunch after the Bible study.

- If we are going to make our small group receptive to prodigals, we have to be willing to go beyond sharing fellowship only with our best friends. Organize events which help people to break out of their convenient cliques.

Church Wide Actions

- Schedule a special "friend day" service that is tailored to guests. Encourage people to bring guests and make sure that the various components of the service are easy to follow for a first time guest.

- Create parking spaces that are close to a main entrance that are clearly and visible marked for guests.

- To assist people in learning how to engage people in the market-place consider scheduling a SPLASH study through your small groups. SPLASH stands for Show People Love And Share Him. It is a six-week study that provides a biblical basis for sharing along with practical helps.

- Recognize and reward people as appropriate for bringing friends with them to church events. This can be done publicly when appropriate, but it is always appropriate to privately affirm people for valuing others as a gift from God.

Have fun looking for prodigals. After all, we too were once in that category.

CHAPTER TWO

Engaging Every Guest with Intentionality

My wife loves to entertain. She looks forward to any and every opportunity to have guests visit our home. I think she makes up holidays just to have another chance to invite someone over for lunch, dinner, coffee, or tea.

The days and hours prior to the visit are sometimes a tiny bit hectic, but generally everything is ready in time. My wife lovingly prepares the home to receive our guests. She vacuums, dusts, and insures that everything is in its proper place. She either cuts flowers from our yard or purchases them if they are not readily available in the yard. She displays them in prominent places where they will be most enjoyed by our guests. Needless to say, we both are involved in the preparation of the home, both inside and out. My task is to mow, edge, and weed so that the yards looks its very best. As we near the deadline, everyone in the family is called upon to do "whatever it takes" to make our guests feel at home.

If we are having a meal together, the table is set and the food is prepared. We always attempt to give our guests the best we can afford. If they are staying the night, we want their room to be fresh and prepared before they arrive. We want them to know that we have been expecting them and we are honored that they chose to visit with us. Further, we want them to have such a delightful visit that they will come again.

When the day of their arrival comes, we greet our guests with a smile and a hug (when appropriate). If we have several guests, I often greet them in the driveway and help them park their vehicle. Our driveway is pretty steep, parking is at a premium, and backing down our driveway is a challenge during the daytime, much less when it is dark. I help them park their car because I don't want a great evening to be spoiled by a challenging adventure trying to negotiate one's way down the drive when other cars are present.

Once the guests have arrived, we invite them into our home, take their coats, and make them feel welcome. If we have a large group, we make sure that everyone is introduced. On some occasions we will actually provide name tags to help people feel comfortable around persons they have just met. We attempt to seat people with someone they will enjoy visiting with. We always give our guests the best seats and serve them first.

Can you identify with any part of this story? Did you notice that everything was done with the guest in mind and with clear intentionality? Every church should strive to treat every guest as a gift from God. In truth, Jesus indicates that when we care for the least of the least, we are actually ministering to Him (Mt. 25:40).

The writer to the Hebrews begins his concluding remarks by reminding his readers to let love of the brethren continue (13:1). Most churches are pretty good at "loving the brethren." But our author immediately follows this command with another one which places Christian hospitality at home or at church in a whole different light. "Do not neglect to show hospitality to strangers, for by this some have entertained angels without knowing it" (Heb. 13:2). Here's a free tip—treat every guest to your church as an angel sent by God and watch what happens.

You may be wondering why we are making such an issue of "engaging every guest with intentionality." Here are four important and undeniable truths. (1) The church is a critical instrument for the advancement of the kingdom and thus Christ has promised to grow His church. (2) Your church will not grow without regular guests. (3) Your church will not grow if your guests don't return. (4) You never get a second chance to make a great first impression.

So, yes, this is an important topic. It is vital to the kingdom and thus it is a priority to kingdom-minded people. So let's pause to see what God's Word has to say about the value of hospitality.

Encountering the Word

One of my favorite Pauline letters is Romans. It was written to prepare the way for Paul's visit to Rome and to solicit the aid of the church in Rome as Paul contemplated an even more expansive mission journey to Spain and beyond (15:24). He was desirous to have the opportunity to preach the gospel in Rome and to be encouraged together with the Roman believers (1:12, 15). Since Paul was not known by sight to the Romans and because he wanted them to support him in his missionary work, he shares a fairly comprehensive outline of his theology. The first eleven chapters read like a systematic theology which explains why many of us first learned to share our faith by means of the Roman Road, a system that moves consecutively through Romans with a simple outline of the gospel.

Beginning in chapter 12, Paul provides practical application based on the theological truths shared in the first eleven chapters. He introduces this section with the twin foundations for all meaningful Christian service. "Therefore I urge you, brethren, by the mercies of God, to present your bodies a living and holy sacrifice, acceptable to God, which is your spiritual service of worship. And do not be conformed to this world, but be transformed by the renewing of your mind, so that you may prove what the will of God is, that which is good and acceptable and perfect" (Rom. 12:1-2).

Everything in the Christian life begins with the presentation of our bodies to God. God is interested in your *availability* and not your *ability*. Many Christians fail to become involved in the ministry of the church because they don't feel *worthy* or *capable*. Did you happen to notice that God declares the gift of yourself to Him as *acceptable*? Since God created you and redeemed you for service to Him, when you offer yourself to Him it is what He desires and all He desires.

The second foundation truth is found in verse two. We are to be transformed by the renewing of our minds. We really only have two options when it comes to the matter of our thinking. We can allow the world to squeeze us into its mold or we can be transformed by the constant renewal of the mind. The world tells us that life is about us and therefore we must "look out for number one" and "grab for the gusto." Such thinking can lead to unhealthy self-gratification. This sort of distorted thinking can cause believers to think that the church was designed for their pleasure and gratification.

On the other hand, the world may tell us we have little or no value to God or anyone else. Such thinking leads to inactivity and apathy. God tells us that we are created in His image, redeemed by His grace, gifted and empowered by His Spirit so that we can join Him as partners in kingdom activity. Do you believe and act upon the truths declared about you by God in His Word? You are children, heirs, fellow-heirs, beloved, salt, and light.

In verses 3-8 Paul gives us a simple overview of his teaching on spiritual gifts. Every believer is gifted by God to serve in and through His body the church for the reaching of the nations. Since the gifts are diverse, the body is composed of many equally important members with different functions based on their giftedness. It is our diversity that demands and enables our unity. Each member has the privilege of serving God through the effective use of his/her gift.

As soon as he has shared the exciting truth about gifted service, Paul looks at the factors that enable uniquely gifted people to live in community together. The overarching theme is found in verse 9—"Let love be without hypocrisy. Abhor what is evil; cling to what is good." The context of all Christian community is "love" which is produced by the Spirit indwelling us. We know that God's love is perfect, self-giving, and undeserved (John 3:16). Because the Holy Spirit now lives in us, we are empowered to love one another with God's love. The purity of God's love demands that we abhor every kind of evil and cling tenaciously to all good.

God's love is first of all expressed in the context of God's family. "Be devoted to one another in brotherly love; give preference to one another in honor; not lagging behind in diligence, fervent in spirit, serving the Lord" (12:10-11). Do you hear the passion in the phrase "devoted to one another"? The book of Acts describes the first believers with this same word. "They were continually devoting themselves to the apostles' teaching and to fellowship, to the breaking of bread and to prayer" (Acts 2:42).

It is always a challenge to "give preference to one another in honor." We tend to want our own way; to have our needs met first. We want to keep our class the way it is, have our kind of music, and enjoy church our own way. Yes giving preference to others is challenging and therefore we are reminded that we don't do so in a grudging way, but with diligence and spiritual fervor. What would happen if we actually took these verses seriously in our small group and in our church?

Please don't miss the final point of verse eleven. As we give preference to others we are actually serving the Lord. This servant-like Spirit is modeled after Christ Himself and thus is the greatest privilege of the believer. If the Lord of lords did not come to be served, but to serve, what must be the attitude of His followers?

Verse twelve provides an interesting triad which reminds us how unnatural such self-giving behavior is—"Rejoicing in hope, persevering in tribulation, devoted to prayer." Sometimes our best efforts at "giving preference" are rejected and therefore we must persevere in doing good with the sure hope that the "good seed of our lives and words" do not return void. But the key to such radical living is our commitment to prayer. Living in community is challenging at best. Reaching pre-Christians can be downright frustrating and we can become so calloused we want to give up. It is easy to forget what we were like before Christ.

Paul reminds us that we are to contribute to the needs of the saints and practice hospitality. We cannot treat these instructions as options and claim to be followers of Christ. Hospitality is the key to assimilation at every level. People are looking for authentic community and if the church would dare to follow the mandates of Scripture we would jettison our Teflon coating in an instant and become like Velcro. The unsaved would be drawn to us like burrs to your hiking socks. Believers would be "linked" into the body of Christ with an unbreakable bond. We would open the front door with natural and effective evangelism and close the back door with assimilation. Like Velcro we would see the hook and loop pattern at work.

Applying the Word

1. What does it mean to present your body as a living sacrifice?

make yourself available to God's leadership

2. What is involved in "transformation by the renewal of the mind?"

Be open to study the Bible and learn what God wants us to do.

3. Do you regularly serve in your small group and church based on a transformed mind? Give examples.

We pray, study and discuss the Bible together

4. How can we learn to base our behavior, our actions, and our service on the truth of God's Word rather than the standards of the world?

By letting God have control of our lives thru Bible study

5. How are Romans 12:9-12 and Hebrews 13:1-2 alike?

We are to love one another and the stranger among us

6. Does the word "devoted" describe the fellowship of your small group and that of your church? *yes*

7. How can it be improved?

By being available to put ourselves out where there is a need

8. Is your behavior and that of your church characterized by selfish demands or selfless love? Discuss with examples.

selfless love, by some many willing to hug and make visitors welcome

9. What would change in your small group and your church if you decided today to "give preference to one another in honor?"

10. What ideas do you have for improving hospitality for your small group and for your church?

having our carpet cleaned and our room more inviting

11. Did any of your ideas include non-Christians or were you thinking primarily in terms of the "brethren," meaning those people already connected with your family? *Both*

Making it Stick

Personal Actions

- Repent for selfish attitudes in your own life that might create a barrier to helping your church become more welcoming for newcomers.

- Each time you enter the church campus, ask God to allow you to assist or encourage someone today.

- View yourself as a full-time "greeter" whether you serve in this ministry or not.

- Look for people who may be new and in need of assistance finding their way around the church.

- Make it a point to speak to as many people as possible, welcoming them and asking how their week has been. Yes, fellow-members need encouragement.

- When you bring a friend to your small group, make sure to introduce them to others and insure they are included in the pre-class conversation.

- What ways can you improve the fellowship of your small group?

Small Group Actions

- Assign someone to be at the entry to welcome newcomers to your class. This person should remain in the area of the door after the class has begun in case a guest is late in arriving.

- Make sure you leave open seats near the entry at the back of the class so that guests will not have to "parade" in front of the class to find a seat.

- Position the chairs in your small group so that late arrivers can enter without making a scene or interrupting the class.

- Consider using name tags so that your guests will feel at home.

- Assist newcomers with any registration procedure you might use to keep up with those who attend your small group.

- Coffee, juice, and light snacks can provide a natural conversation starter. Guests should be invited to join you for a cup of coffee.

- Teach your class to use the term "guest" instead of "visitor." The term "guest" is softer and denotes your desire for them to return, and not just visit one time.

Church Wide Actions

The church is in the hospitality business and thus we must think about our church as we would our home when we are expecting to entertain a guest. The first issue is intentionality. If your church does not have a plan to make guests feel at home, it will not occur by accident. Let's continue with our analogy of a guest coming to your home and break our discussion into three parts—1) Preparing for our guests, 2) Welcoming our guests, and 3) Following up on our guests.

Treat every guest as a gift from God. What is your response when you receive a very special gift from a loved one? You express appropriate gratitude. You handle that gift with great care and love. We should be grateful for every guest and handle them with great care and compassion. Your guests want to know whether they will fit and whether they can find friends at your church.

People come to church looking for a "friend" not a "friendly church." Many churches are friendly to each other, but fail to befriend the guest. Teach your people the "Three Minute Rule." The first three minutes after the service, members intentionally engage in conversation with people they do not know. If only half your congregation followed this idea it would greatly increase your success at making guests feel welcome.

Preparing for guests.

1. Think about your church home. Look at the parking lot

and the building from the standpoint of a first-time guest who is totally unfamiliar with the concept of church. Are your parking lot, building, and small group areas prepared with a guest in mind? Is the building clean and inviting?

2. Establish clearly marked spaces for guests to park near a primary entrance.

3. Assign someone to greet guests in the parking lot and at each entrance.

4. Make sure your "greeters" can help people find their way to any area of the building.

5. Create a simple reception area prominently marked inside each major entry to help guests register for small groups or find the appropriate class for their child. These reception areas should have someone who will guide your guests to the appropriate class for themselves and their children. Don't simply point and give instructions, accompany guests and visit with them as you go.

6. Mark the various areas of the building with guest-friendly language to help them find where to go? For example, the word "sanctuary" may mean one thing to you and quite another to someone unfamiliar with our language. Class names such as "Galileans," "TEL," (in case you didn't know TEL stands for Timothy, Eunice, and Lois) and "Explorers" may make insiders feel warm and fuzzy, but they don't communicate with a guest. Think about marking all small groups with categories such as age classification or topic of study based on your organizational strategy.

7. Lessons and sermons should be used that regularly address what it means to be a "friend." Include practical training as a part of the lesson or sermon. Such simple ideas as look-

ing for someone you don't know, introducing yourself to a stranger, asking how you can help someone, can pay rich dividends for your people and your church. The more prepared you are to receive guests, the more guests you will receive. Expecting guests must become the culture of your church.

Welcoming our guests.

A simple and inexpensive way to begin to make your church more hospitable is to begin a "welcome" or "first impression" ministry or improve your present one. This should be a high priority since you only have one chance to make a good first impression for the King. Choose persons who will represent Christ and His church well. Think about people who have a gift of "hospitality."

1. Greeters should be present at their assigned position twenty minutes before small group study or worship begins.

2. Greeters should have a name tag and should wear it at all times while at their station.

3. Greeters should immediately verify that all needed materials are available. Some churches use greeters to hand out bulletins (if they are used), but it is better for ushers to accomplish this task at the doors to the worship center so that greeters can concentrate on welcoming guests.

4. Greeters should introduce themselves and communicate a warm and caring attitude. If you are at a door, open the door. Say, "Good morning and welcome. We are glad you are here today." Call people by their name once you have been introduced. Greet members as well as guests. If there is someone unfamiliar to you, introduce yourself and ask if you can help them in any way.

5. If is best to station two greeters at each entrance door so that when a guest is being escorted to some location in the church there is still someone at the door to help others. Some churches have a welcome center near each entrance that is well-staffed to guide guests to their appropriate class(es), enabling the greeter to continue his/her assigned task. Be sure to use persons who fully represent the diversity you desire in your church family.

6. Your goal is to make people feel at home. Shake hands and look them in the eyes when you speak to them. Take a personal interest in everyone you greet.

7. Greeters should "be prepared" to answer questions, give directions, or escort guests to a location unless this responsibility is handled by someone in a welcome center. If a welcome center is used, the guest should be taken to the center not pointed to it. Introduce the guest by name.

8. Someone should assist the guest in filling out guest registration information.

9. When a family with young children visits, take the entire family to the preschool or children's classes first so they will be familiar with the building and know where to meet children after Bible study or worship. Many churches have an additional registration process for preschoolers to ensure for safety.

10. Help create a mindset in your church that says every member is a greeter! Do not rely on the greeter ministry to handle all the needs. We cannot allow any of God's gifts (guests) to fall through the cracks. When every member views themselves as a greeter, using their gift of hospitality, your church will have the feel of a big family reunion. This Sunday intentionally look for someone you do not

know and spend the first few minutes after the service visiting with them. By the way, it's okay to greet a member you don't know! In the larger church or the church with multiple services, some people are reluctant to speak to a stranger because they are afraid he/she may be a member they don't know. Your smile, handshake, hospitality and pleasant conversation will make a huge impact on your guests and fellow-members.

Every church needs to welcome guests who attend worship. Many persons, who attend a church on their own, will make this their first event. These persons should have been greeted and assisted in the parking lot, at the entrance to the building, and to the worship center before the service begins. Each church must determine the best strategy for greeting worship guests in their given setting. Don't hesitate to try several ideas until you find what works best for you. Here are a few ideas to consider:

- Have a time during the service when you have an informal plan for allowing people to greet one another. It should not be the very first item on the agenda, since guests may be delayed for several reasons, such as enrolling their child in preschool, etc. Some churches have guests remain seated as members begin the greeting process. This is generally done so that ushers can see guests and provide them with a "welcome" packet. If this process is used, make sure guests are invited to stand and join in the family welcome very quickly. Many first-time guests desire some anonymity.

- Whether you use a printed order of service or not is a matter of personal preference. In either case, make sure that all directions are clear so that a first-timer who is not familiar with your church's worship traditions can fully participate. Everyone who gives an announcement, sings, speaks, etc.

should be introduced or introduce themselves. If video screens are used, participants' names can be printed on the screen. Don't assume that your guests know what is coming next or how to respond. Make them comfortable.

- There are numerous ways to accomplish guest registration and each church must find the one that works best for it. The reason for obtaining guest information is not to grow the church, but to meet every ministry need of our guests and members alike. (a) You can have ushers hand out guest cards, (b) you can have guest cards in the pews and draw attention to them from the pulpit, or (c) you can have a perforated card as part of your order if worship. If you use an order of service with a perforated card, the person welcoming the guests should visibly and audibly tear the perforation with the guests. (d) Some churches register people at a guest reception with the pastor after the service. (e) Other churches register everyone by means of a pew pad. If you choose to use this method, members must be taught the value of signing the pad each week to make it more comfortable for guests to sign the pad. (f) One other option is to use a "connection card" which is integral to the service itself and everyone, including members, is encouraged to fill it out and place it in the offering plate. This card would have basic information such as address, phone number, e-mail address etc. on the front. On the back would be place to indicate prayer concerns, interest in knowing more about the church or small groups, how to have a personal relationship with Christ, and a particular response to the message for everyone. Many churches place sign-up lists on this same card thus relieving congestion in the lobby and simplifying registration for events such as a women's luncheon, a youth outing, or men's prayer breakfast. This sort of card needs to be customized each week so that it contains only the items of interest for that week and the specific response to the message. Any card you use should have space for an e-mail address. Some guests will provide this information on the card even when they are reluctant to give a home address or phone number. This one bit of information will allow you to continue to make contact. (ROL "A" Connection Card)

- The person welcoming the guests should make guests feel both welcome and comfortable. This person sets the tone for the entire welcoming process. If a card is used and guests are asked to fill it out, explain the process, tell them why you desire the information, and invite them to fill out only those sections with which they feel comfortable. They are going to do this anyway, but giving them permission sets a tone of integrity.

- Many churches provide a gift to first-time guests. This can be done at a pastor's reception following the service or by having guests take their guest registration form to the welcome center desk to obtain their gift. If you choose to provide a gift, make it meaningful and personal. Don't be cheap when giving gifts to guests. Every church budget should have adequate resources to enable the church to reach its community and this gift should be considered as part of the process. Most guests don't need a cheap pin or a coffee mug. Some popular gifts are helpful Christian books or homemade items that have some symbolic meaning. Gifts can be distributed at the church or taken to the home of first-time guests.

- If you do a pastor's reception the room should be near the worship center and easy to find. Guests can be invited to leave with the pastor prior to the benediction, helping them to find their way before the crowd leaves. Light refreshments can be provided at a pastor's reception. Make sure there are adequate persons at the reception to serve refreshments, register guests, and provide a gift if one is to be given.

Following up with guests.

Follow up is a simple process designed to say "thank you for coming; we hope you will come again." Follow-up must be immediate to be effective. Your first goal is to turn first-time guests into second time guests. The chance of a first-time guest becoming a regular attendee nearly doubles with each subsequent visit. Some churches have a goal of making seven specific contacts within seven days. Once again, we want to encourage you to be creative and intentional. You don't have to copy any other church's strategy or the ideas suggested here, but you must design a strategy that works for you. A key to follow-up is obtaining adequate information from your guests that will allow you to call, visit, or send an e-mail.

1. If an e-mail address is obtained, send an immediate e-mail thanking your guest for visiting and encouraging them to return or make specific contact. Nelson Searcy (Fusion) suggests using a simple three or four question evaluation that you ask them to return via e-mail. Include questions that are meaningful and will help you provide for the needs of guests. For example, you can ask, "How did you first hear about our church," "Was there adequate visitor parking," "Were you greeted when you entered the building," "Were you made to feel part of the family," "Did you enjoy the service," "Is there any way we can minister to or pray for you or your family"? Make the survey brief and simple

to answer so it can be done on a computer or mobile device.

2. If a physical address is given, have someone go by the home immediately after the service. This person is not to enter the house or make a visit. If the guest is home, they can thank them for attending and indicate that someone will call them to see how the church family can continue to be of service to you or your family. This person can also convey a gift or provide a packet of information about the church.

3. If a phone number is provided, someone should follow-up with a personal call as soon as feasible. It is best for the pastor and staff to make this call to introduce themselves and see if the guest/family have any specific questions after their first visit. This call can also be used to schedule an in-home visit when appropriate. In our culture, most people prefer a scheduled visit rather than one that is unannounced. The caller should indicate that someone from the guest's age group will be visiting to get to know them and answer any questions they might have about our church. Having persons of similar age visit in homes takes advantage of the principle of "homogeneity" which indicates that the gospel flows most rapidly through commonalities.

4. If the guest attended worship only, have someone from the appropriate small group call and give a personal invitation to attend small group Bible study next week. The best invitation is to offer to pick the person up and bring them with you to small group Bible study. If this is not appropriate, offer to meet them in a conspicuous place and take them to the location of the small group.

5. If the guest attended a small group as well as worship, each

small group outreach leader should make a personal call. If the guests had children with them, the children's teacher should make a personal call also. This call should always begin with the parents and speak to the child only with the permission of the parents.

6. A personalized letter should be sent thanking the person for their visit. (ROL "B" Letter)

7. When appropriate an in-home visit should be made by someone from the appropriate age classification. These people should be trained to make a simple gospel presentation when appropriate (this will be covered in more detail in the next chapter). They should also be prepared to answer any question about the church. A primary goal is to get to know the guest on a more intimate basis and see what ministry can be provided for them or their family.

8. Some system must be designed for tracking guests so they are not neglected as time progresses. The best way to do this is to enroll them in a small group which then becomes responsible for their care and nurture (see chapter 6).

I am sure that those who have been tasked with responding to the church-wide area may find this chapter a bit overwhelming. Relax, take a deep breath and ask God to give you the leadership concerning where you should begin. We have given more ideas than any one church can apply to allow you to develop a customized approach that fits your church. We have every confidence that you will find the ideas that will help your church become a Velcro church.

CHAPTER THREE

Leading Our Friends to Christ

I know that the title of this chapter may be intimidating to some readers. You are thinking about the E word—"evangelism" — and just thinking about it is causing your palms to sweat. Take a deep breath and relax. I promise this will not be another guilt-laden message designed to make you feel bad for not doing more to lead friends to Christ. What we are going to discuss is something you can do and that you will enjoy doing.

The E word may conjure up all sorts of images that are unpleasant and threatening. We may think of someone "button-holing" a stranger with the assertion that they must "turn or burn," "get right or get left." We may think that evangelism is too confrontational for our temperament. We may think that to be effective in leading a friend to Christ we have to go through a long process of memorization. The presentation is then the recitation of a string of scriptures followed by a few transition phrases that we recite as quickly as possible so we won't forget the next point in the outline.

Please understand that I have no desire or intention of making fun of anyone's approach to sharing their faith with a friend. I admire anyone who cares enough to make any effort to tell someone about Christ. Further, I know from experience that God can use what we consider to be "feeble attempts" to bring someone to faith in His Son. I simply want to dispel the notion that there is only one way to effectively share one's faith and thus participate in the wonderful privilege of leading a friend to Christ.

Our goal in this chapter is to engage in a Bible study that will help us understand how believers work together to bring friends to Christ. I hope you noticed two things about the title to this chapter. First the pronoun "our" is plural. Most effective evangelistic efforts involve teamwork. Working as a team provides encouragement and partnership that makes evangelism a pleasure and privilege rather than a burden to be borne and a task to be accomplished. Think of evangelism as the privilege of telling someone about your best friend and your greatest discovery. Our part is to share our story of how Christ has changed our lives and then leave the results with God. Remember the truth of 1 Corinthians 3:6-7, "I planted the seed, Apollos watered it, but God made it grow. So neither he who plants nor he who waters is anything, but only God, who makes things grow" (NIV).

The second point of interest in the title is the word "friend." In the first chapter we spoke of *people* you encounter, in the second chapter we spoke of *guests* who come to your small group or church for a visit. Now we are talking about sharing good news with a *friend*. Our goal is to move people step by step to a personal relationship with Christ.

What could be more natural than sharing good news with a friend? Just think about it. You discover a new restaurant that is really good. What is your first reaction? You call a friend because you want them to join in your good fortune.

Those who measure such things tell us that less than 10% of persons who have a personal relationship with Christ have ever told anyone about that relationship. Why do you think that is the case? I don't think any true believer wants their friend, relative, neighbor, or (even) enemy to spend eternity in hell. The problem is that we have created an approach that seems for many to be somewhat artificial, forced, and intrusive. We have made it a program of the church which makes it the "specialty" of a few well-trained, hearty souls. The green beret of the Christian community!

Let's take a few moments to study God's Word together to see what we can learn about friends leading friends to Christ. Hopefully we will discover principles that we can use in our everyday lives.

Encountering the Word

There are numerous stories in the Bible of great friendships. We immediately think of David and Jonathan. Jonathan saved David's life even though it meant standing against his own father. In the New Testament we encounter friendships like those of Paul and Barnabas or Paul and Timothy. Perhaps the best known and most beloved story of friendship in the entire Bible is found in Luke 5 as well as Mark 2. It is the story of four friends who tear open a roof to bring a paralytic friend to Christ.

Let's visit the story in its original context. Luke chapter five begins with the calling of the first disciples. Peter, James, and John are called and commissioned from the bow of their fishing boat as they witness the power of God at work in Jesus. It is clear they understand that Jesus is fully God because of the miracle of the great catch of fish. When we see Peter fall on the ground confessing his sin, he is responding to God in human flesh (5:8). Jesus tells them that they have been chosen to enter a new phase of their fishing ministry—this one for men (5:10). They leave everything and follow Him; the natural response of any disciple.

The activity is fast and furious from this point forward. Jesus heals a man with leprosy, a disease that, in the first century, made an individual an outcast. Jesus, understanding that such powerful miracles would create intense Messianic expectation, tells the leper to tell no one. Nonetheless, the news about Jesus was spreading rapidly and the crowds were growing in size and enthusiasm (Lk. 5:15).

Luke and Mark both give us detailed information about the next event in the life of Jesus. "One day He was teaching; and there were some Pharisees and teachers of the law sitting there, who had come from every village of Galilee and Judea and from Jerusalem; and the power of the Lord was present for Him to perform healing" (Lk. 5:17). At this point, we don't know why the Pharisees and Rabbis are present. Later in His ministry, the religious leaders are often present because they are looking for a way to entrap Jesus. At this point, it may be that they are simply present out of curiosity. Everyone must have been wondering, "Who is this man who has the power to cure leprosy?"

Mark adds detail to the story when he tells us that Jesus was home in Capernaum (Mk. 2:1). The house where He was teaching is not specifically identified, but it is natural to think that it may have been the home of Peter and Andrew (cf. Mk. 1:29). His presence in the city could not be concealed for long and thus word spread that Jesus was at home (2:1). Listen to Mark's description of the setting: "And many were gathered together, so that there was no longer room, not even near the door; and He was speaking the word to them" (2:2).

While Jesus is teaching inside the home; four men approach, carrying a paralytic friend on a stretcher. The size of the crowd gathered to hear Jesus makes it impossible for the men to make a direct approach to Jesus. In grim determination, they ascend a stairway on the side of the house to the flat roof where they dig an opening in order to lower their friend on his pallet before Jesus. Jesus recognizes this bold effort as an expression of faith and He tells the paralytic that his sins have been forgiven.

Jesus' pronouncement of forgiveness must have caught everyone off guard. The four men brought the paralytic for physical healing, which they were convinced that Jesus could provide. But everyone knew that only God could forgive sin. The immediate announcement of forgiveness is made more intelligible if we place it against the Old Testament background where sin and disease and forgiveness and healing were often connected. Healing is often the demonstration of forgiveness in the Old Testament (2 Chron. 7:14, Ps. 103:3, 147:3 and Isa. 19:22). In a number of texts the two words are virtually interchangeable. For example the Psalmist declares, "Heal my soul, for I have sinned against You" (41:4b). Hosea 4:14 speaks of God "healing" Israel's apostasy.

In a very real sense sickness, disease, and death are the consequences of the sinful condition of mankind (Rom. 8:21). For that reason, every healing is the undoing of the impact of sin; it is the gracious activity of God in the sphere of sin at work in the fallen world. One day, when Christ returns in glory, those who have experienced His forgiveness will be fully delivered from the disease and corruption that accompanies all sin (Rev. 21:1-4). We should not, however, attempt to find a corresponding sin for each instance of earthly sickness. This passage contains no suggestion that the suffering of the paralytic was related to any specific sin on his part. The physical healing was a visible example of the power of God in Christ to make man whole.

The scribes, introduced by Mark at this point, were men who were schooled in the written Law and its oral interpretation. They are offended by Jesus' declaration, announcing the forgiveness of sin. The Old Testament is crystal clear that God alone has the authority to forgive sins and they affirm that truth (Mk. 2:7). In Jewish thought, the Messiah would exterminate the godless in Israel and protect His people from the reign of sin, but the forgiveness of sin was not attributed to Him.[1]

Jesus speaks carefully and perhaps somewhat ambiguously—"Son, your sins are forgiven" (Mk. 2:5). Notice in this first instance He does not say that He is providing forgiveness. In the Old Testament, prophets sometimes declared forgiveness that was provided by God. You may recall that Nathan the prophet confronted David with his sin after the affair with Bathsheba and the murder of Uriah. In response to David's repentance, Nathan declared, "The Lord also has taken away your sin; you shall not die" (2 Sam. 12:13). The scribes must have been offended by Jesus' pretention to prophetic office. They therefore accuse Him of blasphemy, a crime punishable by death (Mk. 2:7).

Jesus understands what they are thinking, but rather than arguing with them, He asks them whether it would have been easier for Him to have told the paralytic that his sins were forgiven or to tell him to get up and walk. Logically, no one could see whether forgiveness had occurred or not, but anyone could see if the healing of a paralytic had occurred. Thus the visible evidence, provided by healing, was a visible sign of victory over the Adversary at an invisible and deeper level. Such victory is a clear sign that the sovereign activity of God is seen in what Jesus does. In truth, forgiveness is both the more essential and more difficult of the two actions.

Mark tells us that this early event in the life and ministry of Jesus was a clear, early indication of that which would become clear after the resurrection. The Son of Man (a favorite self-designation of Jesus used over 80 times in the gospels and here in Mark's Gospel for the first time) has authority on earth to forgive sins. This healing, occasioned by the faith of four friends, provides an opportunity for man to see what would become self-evident after the resurrection. Jesus demonstrates that He is more than a prophet, speaking on behalf of God; He is fully God with the power to forgive sins on earth. This truth explains why we are compelled to find a way, even if it means we must figuratively tear the roof off the church, to bring our friends to Christ. Only He can provide the remission for sins.

Applying the Word

1. What risk did the four men take to bring their paralytic friend to Christ?

nothing, It was a act of faith Repair to roof

2. Why do you think the scribes and Pharisees were present?

They were curiosity

3. Both Luke and Mark mention the large crowd of people present. Who do they represent?

People who wanted to hear more about Jesus and why he had the ability to heal

4. Why do you think the scribes and Pharisees show no apparent joy over the healing of the paralytic? *Jesus not only healed but forgave the man of his sins which was consequence of sickness*

Is it possible for believers to behave like scribes and Pharisees in regard to the unsaved? If so, how.

5. How did the crowd inadvertently keep the paralytic from Jesus? *It was so crowed they couldn't get in the door*

Are we ever like the crowd? How? *We often only think of ourselves and want we want*

6. What factors were involved in the decision of the four friends to go to the considerable trouble to bring their friend to Jesus?

They had faith to believe that Jesus could heal the man

7. Do you think the helpless condition of the paralytic played a role? *yes*

What parallels do you see with the condition of friends who do not know Christ?

8. What demonstrates their commitment to never give up in their quest to bring their friend to Christ?

They carried him, cut a hole in the roof and lowed him to Jesus

9. What are the factors that sometimes cause us to give up on our friends?

They are too much trouble and never listen to advise

10. It appears that the actions of the four friends were based on their conviction that Jesus alone could help their friend. What is your basic conviction about Jesus?

He is still the only one who can save us and forgive our sins

Making it Stick

Our goal is to move persons from the category of "people" (those outside the church) to that of "guests" (church contacts) and now to "friends" (fellow-followers) of Jesus. Nine out of ten pastors categorize their church as "evangelistic." The percentage would probably be higher if the same question was posed to most members. Yet, research indicates that a very small percentage of believers have ever told anyone of their relationship to Christ. Now let's see what we can do to change those tragic statistics.

Personal Actions

- List the names of three lost friends who you will pray for by name for the next month.

- Enlist two friends who will agree to join you in praying for these lost friends.

- Take a concrete loving action toward one of these persons during the next couple of weeks. For example, you might give them a Christian book that you believe would be helpful to them and ask if you can discuss the book with them after they read it.

- Seek an opportunity to invite this friend to your home or to a restaurant for a casual meal where you can get to know them better. As you prepare to eat, tell them you would like to pray for the food and ask them how you can pray for them or their family personally.

- Look for an opportunity to bring your friend with you to a small group event or church activity that you believe might be a non-threatening event.

Small Group Actions

- Develop a prayer list for "friends" of the group who are unsaved.

- Have specific times of prayer that these persons will soon come to a saving knowledge of Christ.

- Use the **ABC** approach to praying that Paul recommends in Col. 4 and Eph. 6. Pray first for **A**ccess to an opportunity to present the gospel. Pray for **B**oldness to speak the gospel as you should. Finally pray for **C**larity in your presentation.

- Plan regular pre-evangelism events where members of your small group are encouraged to bring unsaved friends. Use your imagination. Make sure they are fun and non-threatening. Consider a cook-out at the park or a swimming party etc.

- After a pre-evangelism event of this nature, have a specific Sunday where members will be encouraged to bring their friends with them to the small group Bible study.

- Take one small group session and lead persons to mark their Bible with the Roman road plan for presenting the gospel. (ROL "C" Gospel presentation)

- Write out your story and practice sharing it within your small group. Try to use as little "religious language" as possible. This will make it easier for you to share with those outside your small group who are not-yet Christians.

Church Wide Actions

- Establish a climate for natural evangelism by talking about evangelistic opportunities provided by the church.

- Regularly allow time during church wide events for people to share their testimonies of how they came to know Christ.

- Make every decision for Christ a "big event" since the angels in heaven celebrate each conversion. We might as well join the celebration.

- If your church practices baptism for believers, allow those involved with leading someone to Christ, to participate in the baptismal event or be recognized at the event.

- Schedule church-wide events designed to provide an opportunity for members to bring friends who are not-yet followers of Christ. (ROL "D" Church Events)

- Regularly provide numerous ways for people to respond to the invitation to know Christ. You can invite persons to a discovery class, ask them to meet someone after the service who can answer questions about Christ, or join the pastor at the front at the end of the service. There is no one right way to ask people to respond to Christ. Most evangelistic churches provide multiple opportunities to respond.

- Make praying for pre-Christians a priority in every appropriate setting.

- Consider scheduling an evangelistic training event such as SPLASH, Share Jesus Without Fear, or a One Day Witnessing event. The more training you provide the better will be the evangelistic results.

I hope you enjoyed reading the ideas about natural evangelism as much as we enjoyed sharing them with you. I don't think I have ever met a believer who didn't feel the need to be more effecting in sharing their story with a lost friend. I trust these ideas will make your church and your people more effective in the context where God has placed you.

1   William L. Lane, *The Gospel According to Mark* (Grand Rapids, Michigan: William B. Eerdmans Publishing Company, 1974), 95.

CHAPTER FOUR

Connecting to Community

You may recall that we began our study with a look at the discovery and development of Velcro. In the trade world it is referred to as a "hook and loop" fastening system. When two pieces of Velcro are pressed together the myriad of tiny hooks become intertwined with the loops. The more hooks you have in contact with loops, the more secure will be your connection.

The same is true when it comes to your church. The more hooks and loops you put in place to become intertwined with one another the more effective will be the kingdom impact of your church. This in turn will enable your church to grow spiritually and physically. The growth of your church has a direct impact on the number of persons who will have the joy of spending eternity with Christ. This is precisely why Jesus' last command was for the church to make disciples of all the nations. Don't become so bogged down with the details of this book that your forget the ultimate goal.

In the first three chapters, we have looked at:

- the hook side of the equation as we focused on maximizing our contacts with persons in our community.
- the need to engage every guest with intentionality once they have responded to our invitation to visit our small group or church.
- ways to participate in the wonderful process of leading our friends to Christ.

We have been moving *people* from every sphere of our community to become *our guests* at a small group event or church-wide event. In the last chapter we looked at *guests* becoming *friends* of our best friend, Jesus. Notice that the hook element of the Velcro process has been in effect during this entire first phase of our process of connecting people to Christ. In this chapter we are looking at the first loop in the Velcro process. We now want to connect our *friends* to community so that they can become *family.*

Don't lose sight of the fact that our ultimate goal is to secure as many people as possible to Christ and His church so that they may enjoy serving Him for all eternity. *The church is the only earthly organization that will exist for all eternity (Rev. 21:2). Nothing you accomplish through any earthly organization will have the eternal impact of that which you accomplish through the church.*

Encountering the Word

Let's look at the first letter of John. From clues in the letter, it appears that John's first letter was written to a group of churches under attack by false teachers. It is possible that some individuals who had once been associated with the Christian community had adopted heretical doctrine and had left the church (see I Jn. 2:18-28). These false teachers went so far as to organize and send out itinerant teachers who moved among the churches with the goal of sowing discontent and converting members of the churches to their false way of thinking.

Thus this letter has two primary objectives. First, John wants to combat the propaganda of the false teachers. Doctrinally, their teaching attempts to compromise the person and work of Christ. Specifically, John indicates that they were unwilling to confess that Jesus of Nazareth is the Christ (Messiah King) (2:22). Further they deny that Jesus had come in the flesh (4:2-

3). It is likely that these false teachers had been influenced by Gnostic thought. The word "Gnostic" comes from the Greek word *gnosis*, meaning "knowledge." Gnosticism took many forms, but it generally emphasized the essential goodness of spirit and the inherent evil of all matter. Thus they saw Jesus as some type of spirit—believing that a spirit controlled Jesus from His baptism until His crucifixion. They refused, however, to associate the human Jesus with "the Christ." As you might imagine, this faulty view of Christ, led to an equally deficient view of His death.

False teaching, as is always the case, had immediate moral and social consequences. Morally, the false teachers minimized the seriousness of sin (1:6-10). They wanted to claim that one could have fellowship with God regardless of one's behavior. In contrast, John insists that genuine relationship to God will lead to obedience and its concomitant ethical implications. Socially, the spiritual pride of the heretics led to a lack of brotherly love (2:9, 11). John insists that love for the brethren is a manifestation of genuine Christianity (3:14, and 4:7-21).

A second major objective is to reassure believers of their full inheritance. The false teachers had created doubt and confusion among believers. John assures them of the reality of their faith so that they might know that they have eternal life (5:13). John addresses Christian assurance from both an objective and a subjective perspective. Objectively, the historical events of Christ's life and work were observed by eyewitnesses and passed on to them faithfully (1:1-3). Subjectively, they know that their lives have been transformed through faith in Christ.[1]

With this historical context in mind, let's turn our attention to several key verses in chapter one. John's letter begins with a prologue rather than a salutation. If you read this prologue and the one in John's Gospel, you will find several striking similarities. Both go back to "the beginning" and both emphasize "Word," " Father," and "Life." Since the writing of the letter actually precedes the writing of the gospel, it is likely this prologue forms the basis for the more elaborate one in John's Gospel.

The prologue speaks of the Word of Life which we have heard, seen, and touched. The Word of Life which was manifested to us was always with the Father and is by definition "eternal." Since only God is eternal in nature, only He can give eternal life. Eternal life, which was always with the Father, was made manifest to man through the incarnation. The gospel is anchored in eternity but made manifest in time by means of the incarnation. When God became flesh in Jesus Christ the eternal was united to the historical. This emphasis on the incarnation dealt a death blow to the teachings of Gnosticism which despised and denied the flesh.

John declares that such profound and precious truths must be shared. "What we have seen and heard we proclaim to you also, so that you may have fellowship with us; and indeed our fellowship is with the Father, and with His Son Jesus" (1:3). One cannot experience the gospel and then fail to proclaim it. No one should keep such good news to himself/herself.

Did you happen to notice the repetition of the word "fellowship" in verse 3? If you read ahead through the rest of the chapter, you will find this word occurring with great frequency. The proclamation of the gospel is the way to fellowship (1:3). Today in many churches "fellowship" is sometimes promoted in an unhealthy and introverted fashion. What we speak of as fellowship is often more akin to cliquishness. Some people fear their church will become so large they will "lose their fellowship." Because of this fear, they fail to reach out to the community. Underline this truth-- you do not lose fellowship through numerical growth-- you actually enhance it. When we declare the gospel we expand our fellowship and our joy (1:3-4).

We do not have an adequate English word to translate the Greek word *koinonia*, which is usually translated as "fellowship" or "communion", but the true meaning is much richer and broader. In Luke 5:10 this word is used to speak of joint owners of a fishing boat. We might use the term "partnership" to speak of joint ownership today. In other contexts, it can convey ideas such as "oneness in community," "something held in common," or "common participation or sharing in something."

Our *koinonia* is unique in that it has both a human component as well as a divine component. Did you notice that John first indicates that believers proclaim truth to unbelievers so that they may have "fellowship with us?" He then immediately adds, "Indeed our fellowship is with the Father, and with His Son Jesus Christ" (3). The only way to enhance and expand fellowship is to proclaim the gospel to those who do not yet have fellowship with the Father.

In the last chapter we discussed *Leading a Friend to Christ.* We are compelled to share our faith with a friend because we know they can enjoy "fellowship," "partnership," " communion" with the Father and with His Son. But fellowship with God will of necessity be expressed in fellowship with others who are in partnership with God. Any claim to a vital relationship with God that does not manifest itself in genuine human fellowship is a fraud. Christianity does not allow for any notion of a "Lone Ranger" believer. When we are born again, we are born into God's family. This is why it is so critical that we take another step in our Velcro process and connect our *friend* to our community because they are now *family*. Do not underestimate the biblical and practical value of church membership in the process of assimilation.

Any human fellowship that is not grounded in divine fellowship is but a hollow copy of the fellowship that is available to the body of Christ (the church). People can be in the same room and be focused on the same agenda, but still not have genuine fellowship. Genuine fellowship has its foundation in the fellowship two or more believers have with the Father and with His Son.

John concludes his prologue with a simple and yet profound declaration—"These things we write, so that our joy might be made complete" (1:4). The use of the plural "we" speaks of the inclusive fellowship the eyewitnesses to Christ now enjoy with those who have believed because of their witness. The use of "joy" may point to Jesus words recorded in John 15:11 and 16:24. If you take a moment and look at the context of those passages, you will find that this "promised joy" would be the result of abiding in Christ, asking and receiving in prayer, and bearing much fruit, which is defined as loving one another just as Christ loved them (Jn. 15:10, 12-13).

Returning to our focal passage, we can see that joy is the result of fellowship with others who enjoy fellowship with the Father and the Son. Thus the broader the scope of "fellowship," the greater will be the experience of "joy." When we declare Christ and connect others to the body of Christ, the magnitude of our joy increases along with the breadth of our fellowship.

Since our earthly fellowship is a mirror of the fellowship expressed by the unity of the Godhead, John turns to the matter of Light and darkness—images for sin and righteousness. The fundamental truth is that God is Light without any darkness. John focuses on God's character to further define the nature of Christian fellowship and thus the character of those who participate in it.

If one claims to have fellowship with God and habitually walks in the darkness of death, he/she is living a lie (1 John 1:6). When a person is truly "born again," he/she receives the Holy Spirit who bears the fruit of the Spirit—the character of Christ—in his/her life. As persons of the Light, Christians can no longer be comfortable walking in sin. The beautiful truth of our walk is articulated in verse 7—"But if we walk in the Light as He Himself is in the Light, we have fellowship with one another, and the blood of Jesus His Son cleanses us from all sin."

When you read verse 7 aloud, does anything stand out? Verse 6 speaks about persons who claim to have fellowship with God and yet walk in darkness. Verse 7 then speaks of the result of walking in the Light. We would have expected the result to be "fellowship with God," but instead John says we will have "fellowship with one another." The believers fellowship with God and with his fellow-believer is so integrally connected that one's communion with the Father will always be mirrored in his/her communion with other believers.

The only barrier to true Christian fellowship with God and with our fellow-believer is sin—unconfessed and unforgiven sin. For that reason we cannot fall into the false deception that would claim "I am without sin" (8). What then is the solution to sin that disrupts our fellowship with God and with others? "If we confess our sins, He is faithful and righteous to forgive us our sins and to cleanse us from all unrighteousness" (9). Do you think God is serious about the fellowship among the members of His body?

A Quick Look at Two Important Passages

Let's quickly look at two other passages of Scripture, one which shows how each believer is connected to the body of Christ and the other which describes the unique quality of Christian fellowship. In 1 Corinthians 12:13 Paul writes, "For by one Spirit we were all baptized into one body, whether Jews or Greeks, whether slaves or free, and we were all made to drink of one Spirit." Not only are we born again through the agency of the Spirit, we are "immersed" or "baptized" into the body of Christ—the church. It is natural that when one is born again by the Spirit, he/she is placed into a family by that same Spirit.

Later in that same passage Paul declares, "But now God has placed the members each one of them, in the body, just as He desired" (12:18). We often talk about choosing a church home because of the programs, etc., but the truth is God has chosen you for His church and has placed you there by design. Membership in the church is not about privilege, but about service. This entire passage is about spiritual gifts. Every member of every church is gifted by God and placed into the body with intentionality. Part of the Velcro process is to help each member find their place of gifted service. When members feel needed, they are unlikely to drop out.

Acts 4:32-35 gives us a beautiful picture of the caring nature of Biblical fellowship. The people are described as being of "one heart and soul," a phrase we might use for a married couple. Individual members understood that everything they owned belonged to God and therefore they willingly shared with anyone who had need. Luke declares, "For there was not a needy person among them" (4:34a). The generous quality of true fellowship was a testimony to the power of the resurrection (4:33). Is there any evidence in your church that you are living in the power of the resurrection? Is your church a "no need church?"

Applying the Word

1. According to verses 1 and 2 of 1 John, why are we qualified to share the Word of Life?

We are believers. We've seen it, heard it, we have it reveal to you

2. Why do you think John speaks of fellowship as both human and divine?

fellowship with God and each other

3. What is it that makes our joy complete?

fellowship with God and with another

4. According to verse 7, what is the result of walking in the Light?

fellowship with one another & Jesus

5. What is the single most important barrier to fellowship in the local church and what must we do about it?

sin.

6. According to 1 Cor. 12:13, how do we become part of the body of Christ?

By being saved By being Baptized

7. If God has placed you in the church according to His design, do you know what you are designed to do? Why or why not?

8. How does your church measure up with the description of the church in Acts 4? Discuss similarities and differences.

none

9. What steps can be taken to move your church towards an Acts 4 model?

10. If the Bible consistently speaks of the importance of Christian community, why is church membership not highly valued today?

Making it Stick

Personal Actions

- If you have not yet joined the church, why not make that a personal priority.

- Is there someone you know who needs to be connected to the body through membership. Visit them and give them your testimony concerning the value of belonging to Christ's body. Be prepared to share with them truths you learned from this Bible study.

- Do you know your place in the body? Do you know what you are gifted to do? Ask a mature Christian friend, what they think your gift might be. See if your church offers a gift assessment inventory. Sometimes the best way to discover your gift is through trial and error. Try several different areas of ministry and ask the Father to show you where you fit.

- Are you involved in improving the fellowship of your church by meeting practical needs? Who do you know who has a need? Do something today to help meet that need.

Small Group Actions

- Discuss ideas of how you can help friends in Christ become fully-committed members of the church.

- If there are still questions about the value of the church and the necessity of membership, you might want to follow this study with the twelve-week study, *Connected Community: Becoming Family through Church*. See Auxanopress.com for discount prices.

- Organize your small group to meet practical needs of members. For example, you can take meals to the home when there is a sickness. For younger families the offer to help with the children during a time of crisis is a great ministry. The care ministry of the class (chapter 6) is the best way of organizing your class for meaningful activity.

- Give every member an opportunity to serve in your class. Every class should have care leaders, prayer leaders, a recording secretary, teachers, and persons who plan for fellowships. This structure provides for numerous opportunities for service. Consider developing a mentoring program in your class to help new believers find their place of service.

Church Wide Actions

- Consider a church wide study of *Connected Community* to emphasize the importance of church membership.

- Provide exploration classes for those who are considering church membership. Here are some suggestions for the content of an exploration class. Explain your church's vision. Your vision statement answers the question, "why do we exist?" Share your strategies for carrying out your vision. Include your core beliefs/theology, a presentation of the gospel, and a brief history of your church.

- Regular invitations should be given for people to become a member of the church. This can be during the invitation at the end of any worship service or at the end of your exploration or 101 membership class.

- Every church should have a new members' class for everyone who joins the church. This will insure that each person finds their place of community and service. This class should cover the commitment of the church to the member and the expectations of the church for the new member. Share the benefits and responsibilities of being a member, how your church is structured, and how decisions are made (church polity). Challenge all new members to find a place of service based on their spiritual giftedness. Share ministry opportunities, how to get involved in a ministry, and what their next step is as a member.

- We recommend that anyone who joins the church and is not already involved in a small group should be enrolled as part of their commitment to join the church.

- The church should regularly teach about spiritual gifts and help people to discover them through several different means. (ROL "E" Spiritual Gifts)

- The church should organize itself to meet practical needs of all members. This should be an aggressive approach that utilizes the small group structure as the basis of the caring ministry. Every church should strive to be a "no need" church. We recommend the structure discussed in chapter 6.

The actions accomplished through the ministry of the church will have eternal impact. As church members fully comprehend the potential they have to have an eternal impact through the church, they will be more motivated to become involved in their gifted area of service. Nothing we do has the eternal impact of that which we do through the church.

---

1   This introductory material is paraphrased from Daniel L. Akin, *The New American Commentary* (1,2,3 John) (Nashville: Broadman and Holman Publishers, 2001), pp. 28-30.

CHAPTER FIVE

Recognizing Relationships as the Key to Assimilation

Both authors were privileged to serve First Baptist Norfolk when it was experiencing exponential growth. The explosive growth of that church was absolutely a "God Thing" and none of the staff would be so bold as to take credit for what happened as Norfolk grew from around 380 in average attendance to around 2,200 average attendance in the Sunday school small groups.

The growth was exhilarating and humbling at the same moment. It was exciting to see God work through human instruments in such a powerful and effective manner. One of the reasons for our rapid growth was that our people regularly brought friends and neighbors to small group Bible study and church. The atmosphere was nearly electric as people greeted one another, sometimes with a warm embrace, and then introduced their friend to others in the parking lot, hallways, and lobby.

I would be less than honest if I didn't tell you that our rapid growth created numerous challenges. The land owned by the church was inadequate for our needs and therefore we were quickly out of building space and out of parking. We responded to these challenges by implementing multiple opportunities for worship and small group Bible study. While this strategy helped to solve our space problems, it created unique challenges to our fellowship.

We were continually creating new units which meant that people who had been together for a period of time were asked to help start a new small group. But beyond that, some small groups were asked to move to a new time period to provide space for additional small groups to be formed. We were thrilled that God continued to use our church to advance His kingdom by reaching the lost, but we didn't want to sacrifice the warm fellowship our people had come to enjoy. Our church was a "friendly" church. People loved to "hang out" with each other and this fellowship was a key to our rapid growth. As we addressed this issue as a church family, we came to believe—based on our understanding of 1 John 1—that fellowship could never be diluted by numerical growth. Thus we knew we had to address the concern from both a biblical and functional standpoint.

One part of our biblical solution was to preach a series of messages on the church. Several of those messages addressed the issue of fellowship. After one of those messages, I was walking through the lobby observing the animated hugs and joyous conversations as people welcomed one another. A young mother, who didn't look quite as happy as most people, pulled me aside indicating her desire to talk.

Gesturing at the people in the lobby, she said, "Do you know how your sermon made me feel?" Both her tone and her visage told me that this wasn't going to be the typical "wonderful message pastor" salutation. I indicated that I did want to know how she felt. She then explained that the message coupled with the apparent "friendliness" of the lobby made her feel even more alone. She was married, but her husband did not attend church with her. She was shy and thus reluctant to interject herself into one of the animated huddles gathered in the lobby. The "friendliness" of our church that did not include her made her feel that something must be wrong with her.

Here is a profound truth. People aren't looking for a friendly church! They are looking for a friend! The conversation with that young mother caused me to rethink both the message and the structural issues of our church to ensure that, to the best of our ability, we would never again have anyone feel "alone in the crowd." This woman was a member of our church and yet she felt like an "uninvited guest" in her own home. Everyone must establish several meaningful relationships in the church, if they are going to be Velcroed to the church.

The explosion of various "social networking" sites such as Facebook, Twitter, LinkedIn, online dating services, and blogs indicates the need and desire for relationships. The truth is these internet substitutes have not produced authentic personal connectivity which has led to close friendships. Many people live with few if any real friendships and thus experience both personal and spiritual isolation.

George Gallup has reported that Americans are among the loneliest people in the world. We would immediately respond, "These people need the Lord and His church. They need to experience authentic biblical relationships." But here is the problem! Brad Waggoner, in his book *The Shape of Faith to Come* states: "Less than a third of our churchgoers could confidently affirm they have high-quality relationships with fellow church members."[1]

Casual contacts and surface relationships do not Velcro people to the church. We must intentionally connect people to people so that they experience high quality relationships.

Encountering the Word

I am a fan of the Pauline letters because they are brutally honest and amazingly practical. Each letter was addressed to a specific church and intended to bring encouragement and correction. One of the longest of the Pauline letters was sent to the church at Corinth. Even the casual reader immediately recognizes that this church was anything but boring. Issues as diverse as the meaning of spiritual gifts, appropriate sexual behavior, and the eating of idol meat are addressed. One of the underlying issues that had caused many of the problems was "spiritual arrogance" that led some in the community to believe that they were more spiritual than other community members. As you might imagine, this had negatively impacted interpersonal relationships and thus the unity of the church.

We can see the depth of Paul's concern in the opening chapter of 1 Corinthians where Paul mentions that he has heard about the quarrels in the church associated with various leaders. "Now I mean this, that each one of you is saying, 'I am of Paul,' and 'I of Apollos,' and 'I of Cephas,' and 'I of Christ.' Has Christ been divided? Paul was not crucified for you, was he? Or were you baptized in the name of Paul?" (1:12-13). Paul insists that such divisive behavior was actually an indication of their spiritual immaturity (3:1-4). The factions in Corinth were so pronounced that fellow members were unable to enjoy the Lord's Supper together (11:17-22).

One cause of disunity was a misunderstanding of spiritual gifts. Some members of the church saw certain spiritual gifts as "signs" of spiritual ascendancy. Such a distorted understanding of the purpose of the gifts actually undermines the effectiveness of the gifted church since the proper function of the gifts depends on the unity of the community which, in turn, depends on relationships among various members.

Let's take a brief look at 1 Corinthians 12 as we consider the importance of relationships as the "loops" for the Velcro process. We won't have time to look at every verse in this chapter and thus we are going to focus primarily on the issues relevant to our topic.[2]

Paul makes two immediate corrections to the notion that spiritual gifts prove anything about one's spirituality. Two different Greek words are used in verse one and verse four for "gifts." The first is *pneumatika* from the Greek word for "spirit" and the second is *charismata* from the Greek word for "grace." The first was probably preferred by those in Corinth who thought that gifts proved that they were spiritually elite. Paul prefers the word *charismata* which emphasizes the gracious nature of all gifts. Since gifts are by their very nature an expression of God's gracious activity, they tell us nothing about the possessor but everything about the giver. God has graciously gifted each member of His body to accomplish a unique task for the advance of the kingdom.

The second corrective is found in verse 3. The focus in this verse is on the declaration—"no one can say, 'Jesus is Lord' except by the Holy Spirit." "Jesus is Lord" was an early confession of faith that indicated that one had become a follower of Christ. No one could make this confession of faith unless they were empowered by the Holy Spirit to do so, for He is the one who enables us to cry out "Abba! Father!" He testifies with our spirit that we are children of God (Rom. 8:15-16).

Read 1 Corinthians 12:4-12 slowly and underline the words "varieties" "another" and "same." What did you discover? Paul establishes a simple but profound truth. God gives a variety of gifts to different persons but it is the same Spirit at work in every gift, ministry, and effect. All are given for the good of the body. Here is Paul's summary—"But one and the same Spirit works all these things, distributing to each one individually as He wills" (12:11).

In the next two verses Paul compares the unity of the church to Christ. The many members are necessary to form one unified body. Once again the relationships that create unity and its accompanying fellowship are the work of the Spirit. "For by one Spirit we were all baptized into one body, whether Jews or Greeks, whether slaves or free, and we were made to drink of one Spirit" (12:13). The word "baptized" means "immersed" and was probably a reminder of the day each one of them confessed Christ and was baptized in water.

This physical expression of baptism is an outward sign of an inward reality. Not only does it symbolize our death to self and resurrection to new life, it also indicates our immersion into the corporate body of Christ. This is the last mention of "Spirit" in this chapter and is an important bridge to allow Paul to discuss the work of the Spirit in unifying the many members of the body. This is wholly consistent with Paul's teaching that the gifts were given to *each member* for the good of the *whole body* (12:7). Those who thought gifts proved them to be spiritual would clamor for the gifts that drew attention to them, while those who understood that gifts were for the good of the body would seek those most appropriate for edifying the church.

Verses 14 through 26 contain an extended illustration of the working of the human body. Paul's use of a familiar image is striking because the examples often verge on the ridiculous and humorous. The phrase "for the body is not one member, but many" (14) sets the tone of the passage. The zeal to be alike in possessing the spectacular gifts had resulted in the failure to appreciate the diversity demonstrated by members possessing different but less visible or audible gifts. Further, it had created a rampant individualism with each member clamoring for their own rights without concern for the good of the whole.

The foot and the ear are first pictured as insisting that they are not part of the body because they are not the hand or the eye. What a foolish argument. Each is important precisely because it performs a different but equally vital function. The argument among differently functioning body members reminds one of the childhood arguments heard on the playground at recess. "If I can't pitch, I'll take my ball and go home!" Childhood games are precisely that—childish. They were silly but not dangerous. When we play such games in church, they are dangerous because they are detrimental to the cause of Christ in advancing the kingdom.

I asked my good friend Scott to read this book in a rough draft form. Scott is a godly man and a great Sunday school teacher who just happens to be a quadriplegic. In commenting on this section, Scott wrote: "I cannot read 1 Corinthians 12 without thinking about the quadriplegic body. My body is a perfect example of what can happen to the body of Christ if it becomes disconnected from its head. It demonstrates what can happen if a finger tries to be a tongue or a dominant personality who happens to be a nose gathers a huge following of people who want to be noses. It demonstrates what can happen if a large group of members simply sit in the pew and become atrophied through non-use. Atrophy is ugly. My hands have not listened to my head in 31 years and they have become useless and deformed. The body parts I can use have tried to take up the slack for the body parts that are no longer part of the team. The useful body parts are exhausted and on a regular basis go AWOL. When my body parts that are still connected to my head choose to ignore those disconnected 'members' my entire body becomes spastic."

Scott bravely gives us a picture of life as a quadriplegic to shout out a warning to the church. We cannot be disconnected from the head nor can we be separated from one another. Every church member who sits in the pew without using the gift God gives them begins to suffer from atrophy and becomes dysfunctional in the body. A word of warning we must heed. For the architect of the church is none other than the creator of the universe and each of us.

We admire the architect who can design a building that is both beautiful and functional. The church was designed by the Master Architect and He placed you in His body according to His own design and purpose. "But now God has placed the members, each one of them, in the body, just as He desired" (18). In case you are so "humble" you think this verse applies to everyone but you, notice that the phrase "each one of them" actually interrupts the flow of the sentence. God wanted you to understand that no one is in His body by chance. By the grace and gifting of God you are created, redeemed, and gifted to serve with other members of the body to advance His kingdom on earth.

This verse not only rules out the "I'm-not-important-to-the-body" attitude, it also provides a correction for the "I-don't-need-others" attitude that keeps people from becoming involved in the service of their church. When someone asserts their independence from the body they are ignoring the desire and design of the Creator. We are not independent, we are interdependent. We need one another to function properly as Christ's body.

The imagery of the body is pressed even further to illustrate the necessity of relationships among body members in the church. Listen! "If they were all one member, where would the body be? But now there are many members, but one body. And the eye cannot say to the hand, 'I have no need of you'; or again the head to the feet, 'I have no need of you'" (12:19-21). Even members who might be viewed as weaker or less honorable are vital to the ministry of the body (22-24).

It is likely that "weaker" and "less honorable" are best understood in light of some in Corinth who view the spectacular gifts as most vital and impressive. Since the purpose of all gifts is the edification of the body, the true criterion for measuring any gift is its usefulness in the growth of the body and the glorification of the King. There are no useless appendages and no unseemly ones when all work together for the King. Again, the emphasis is on God's design in composing the body with His own purposes in mind (24).

His design mandates, "...that there may be no division in the body, but that the members may have the same care for one another. And if one member suffers, all the members suffer with it; if one member is honored all the members rejoice with it" (25-26). When the body functions properly with all members working in harmonious relationship, mutual care (25) and total empathy (26) will permeate the church. As members of the same body, we are so closely bound together that we share the same feelings.

Paul hammers home the importance of relationships with a final reminder—"Now you are Christ's body, and individually members of it" (12:27). When we neglect or harm one another, we are in essence harming Christ. Do you remember what the resurrected Lord said to Saul when he was persecuting Christians? "Saul, Saul, why are you persecuting Me?" (Acts 9:4). When Paul persecuted a follower of Christ, he was actually persecuting Christ.

It is at this point in 1 Corinthians 12 that Paul expands the initial gift list by adding gifts of leadership as well as gifts of helps and administration. Those people who serve behind the scenes are also gifted. The gift lists are simply intended to illustrate the sort of activities God has designed for the edification of His church. Don't worry if you don't find yourself on a particular list, find your place of service in the church and get involved. The gifts are designed to enable us to join with other believers in work that has an eternal impact. They cannot function without harmonious relationships among all the body members.

Have you noticed that the very design of the body demands close interpersonal relationships among all the members? How then do we allow the Spirit to forge diverse members into a unified whole?

Applying the Word

1. Why are factions such as those indicated by the assertions "I am of Paul" or "I am of Apollos" so detrimental to the church?

spiritual arrogance - some thinking they are more spiritual than others

2. Why does Paul choose to use the word "charismata" as his term for describing the gifts?

It emphasizes the gracious nature of all gifts

3. What is the significance of the confession "Jesus is Lord" in verse 3 and what does it have to do with relationships in the church?

It was the empowed by the Holy Spirit. We are all equal in Gods sight.

4. Why are a variety of gifted members necessary in the church?

Because there are different needs within the church and each one is of equal importance

5. What two things does baptism signify?

death to self and resurrection to a new life (a immersion into the corporate body of christ

6. Why does Paul use the imagery of the human body? What points does he make concerning the church?

gifts were given to each member for the good for the whole body

7. What is the significance of the truth that God has placed each member in the body (12:18)?

no one is in this Holy body by chance It was by Grace we were gifted to serve one another

8. Why do we need each other in the body of Christ?

we need each other to function properly as Christ Body.

9. Are the relationships in your small group and church so intimate that you share the same feelings?

I believe this is true in the fellowship class

10. How are we harming Christ when we fail to establish Velcro relationships in our church?

We miss opportunity to seek out new members and give them a chance to become a Believer

Making it Stick

Personal Actions

- Research indicates that newcomers who remain in church

more than six months have an average of seven good friends in their church.[3] List seven persons whom you consider to be close friends in your church.

- If you could not list seven persons, what can you do to build a friendship network?

- Who do you know in your small group or your church family who seems to be unconnected?

- What can and will you do to ensure that these people are Velcroed to the church?

- Do you know your place in the gifted body? Do you know what you are gifted to do? Ask a mature Christian friend what they believe your gift to be? See if your church offers a gift assessment inventory. Sometimes the best way to discover your gift is through trial and error. Try several different areas of ministry and ask the Father to show you where you fit in His body.

Small Group Actions

- Ask small group members to share their findings about their seven friends and those they indicated might be in danger of being lost to the church because they are disconnected.

- Plan an event where small group members can invite their "unconnected" friends.

- Make sure that your small group has an adequate record system to ensure that no one falls between the cracks and thus becomes disconnected.

- Teach a Bible study on spiritual gifts and allow individuals in the class to affirm the gifts and abilities that they see and appreciate in the lives of others.

Church Wide Actions

- Adopt a record keeping system that will enable you to know who is attending worship and small groups on a regular basis.

- Devise a strategy for reaching out to those whose attendance is sporadic and those whose attendance is declining in regularity.

- Have an intentional strategy for regularly starting new groups for newcomers and present members who have not yet found a place in a small group. The more small groups that you have, the greater will be the probability of involvement.

- Ensure that one in five of all small groups are two years old or less. Research shows that 90% of groups lose their ability to incorporate new people after two years. Small groups encounter a saturation point.[4]

- Find a tool that works in your setting to help people discover their gifts and find a place of service. People involved in meaningful service will be retained. Meaningful service is the most effective form of Velcro.

- Have regular fellowship events which assist people in building Velcro relationships. (ROL "G" Fellowship Events)

- Regularly evaluate how your church is doing in utilizing the four principles of retention.
    - Explain the basic expectations.
    - Ensure small group involvement.
    - Maximize events which help people build relationships.
    - Help people find their place of service.

Lots of great ideas here, don't you think? Ask the Father to show you where to begin. Perhaps you are already doing many of these things and you simply need to do them with greater intentionality. Remember we are in this for the long haul. View this as a distance race and not a sprint.

1   Brad Waggoner, *The Shape of Faith to Come: Spiritual Formation and the Future of Discipleship* (Nashville: B&H Publishers, 2008), p. 236.

2   If you desire a more detailed study of the various texts related to spiritual gifts, you might enjoy *You Are Gifted: Your Spiritual Gifts and the Kingdom of God.* Study guides and video materials are available to accompany the trade book. See AuxanoPress.com.

3   Yeakly, Flavil R., *Why Churches Grow* (Broken Arrow, OK: Christian Communications, Inc. 1979), p.53-55.

4   Arn, Win, *The Pastor's Manual of Effective Ministry* (Monrovia CA: Church Growth, 1990), p.70.

CHAPTER SIX

Organizing Small Groups for Ongoing Care

The fellowship experienced by Christians living in community should foreshadow and create a longing for the eternal community we will experience in heaven. In heaven our joy will be perfected; unsullied by sin, grief, or sadness. In our present experience of community where joy is still mixed with pain and suffering, pain becomes bearable and joy becomes sweeter because they are shared with members of our family. It is this mutual sharing of both pain and joy that knits us to those who have become members of our heavenly family while we yet live on earth. So our pain and suffering is divided and our joy is multiplied.

Does that sound too good to be true? Does it sound too much like preacher-speak? Every time I read the book of Acts, it creates a longing in my heart for true community and it gives me hope that such community is both our calling and our heritage. God, who designed us for community, has also promised to create it and sustain it by His Spirit.

The resurrected Lord counseled His first century followers not to leave Jerusalem until they had received the promised Spirit (Acts 1:4-5). In response they "with one mind" devoted themselves to prayer as they waited for the empowering of the Spirit (Acts 1:14). On the day of Pentecost they again were all together in one place (Acts 2:1). Are you beginning to notice a common thread? You can't experience true community without spending time with one another. Believers must be in one place and with one mind.

At this point in his narrative, Luke tells us that the Spirit comes in great power, enabling the gospel to be preached with such power that people from the surrounding nations were able to hear it in their own language (Acts 2:8) and about three thousand souls were added to the community of believers (2:41). The powerful preaching of the gospel is not the end of the story concerning the work of the Spirit. "They were continually devoting themselves to the apostles' teaching and to fellowship, to the breaking of bread and to prayer. Everyone kept feeling a sense of awe; and many wonders and signs were taking place through the apostles. And all those who had believed were together and had all things in common" (2:42-44). The creation of community was as much a work of the Spirit as was the conversion of 3,000.

Many commentators, church growth authors, and pastors have looked to this passage to define the essential elements of the work of the church. They point to matters such as doctrinal teaching, prayer, worship, fellowship, and evangelism as the five core functions of the church. However, too little attention has been paid to the fact that without community, the other elements will not be sustained. If we are not "devoted" to fellowship, there will be no foundation or gathering where prayer, worship, and doctrinal instruction can flourish.

Luke gives us another glimpse at the importance and impact of community in Acts 4:32. He describes the believers as being of one heart and soul (Acts 4:32). This was not sentimental rhetoric. The early believers didn't cling to anything as if it was their own but freely shared with any who had need (4:33 and 34). The impact was such that "there was not a needy person among them" (4:34). The unique fellowship of the early church bore testimony to the resurrection of the Lord Jesus and gave evidence that His grace was upon them all (4:33). In other words, *effective evangelism* is dependent on *visible community*. The world is longing for authentic community and the church which dares to provide it will flourish in terms of evangelism and assimilation.

This level of fellowship will not occur simply because we long for it. It will not occur by accident. While community is the work of the Spirit, it demands human cooperation. God is not a God of confusion, but one of order (1 Cor. 14:33). We must organize through our small groups and then work the process. We suggest you apply the "**ISSE**" formula. You need an **I**ntentional plan which is **S**ustainable, **S**imple, and **E**xpandable. Once again we find such a strategy in God's Word as we turn together to Exodus 18.

Encountering the Word

Israel has miraculously escaped from Pharaoh's grasp and has begun their journey to the Promised Land. They experience God's provision as they encounter and overcome roadblocks on the way to their new home. This group of former slaves defeats the mighty Amalekite army at Rephidim. Victory is assured as Moses holds the staff of God aloft. As the battle progresses, Moses becomes weary and Aaron and Hur support his arms. Leadership is a heavy burden and thus must be shared with others.

Following this great military victory, Jethro, the priest of Midian and Moses' father-in-law, comes to visit. By now, every nomad in the peninsula would have heard of the Israelite escape from Pharaoh and victorious battle with Amalek (18:1). Jethro brings Moses wife and two sons, who had been sent to Midian for their own safety during the time of battle.

The scene in verse 7 is typical of eastern courtesy as Moses bows down before his father-in-law and embraces him warmly and kisses him on both cheeks. Jethro is taken into Moses' tent where he hears the account of all that God has done in delivering them from the Pharaoh and providing for them during their journey.

Not only does Jethro rejoice in all that God has done, he confesses the God of Israel as supreme over all gods. "Now I know that the Lord is greater than all the gods; indeed, it was proven when they dealt proudly against the people" (18:11). Yahweh, the one true God, has demonstrated His sovereignty by His saving activity. Jethro, as a new convert, leads in providing a burnt offering expressing thanksgiving. He then joins the elders of Israel as they share in a communal meal, feasting in the presence of the Lord (18:12).

The celebration of victory lasts only one day and then Moses feels compelled to return to the arduous task of judging the people. The size of the task is clearly seen as the text indicates that the people stood before him from morning until evening. In patriarchal days, justice was dispensed by the clan chieftain. As slaves in Egypt, the Israelites had not developed a judicial system of their own and therefore Moses was left to arbitrate all disputes.

Seeing the enormity and impossibility of the job Moses bore alone, Jethro approaches him expressing concern. "What is this thing that you are doing for the people? Why do you sit as judge and all the people stand about you from morning until evening?" (18:14). Moses replies that they come before him because he is God's representative and they desire to inquire of the Lord. Moses regards his judicial task as an opportunity for teaching and thus, rather than simply dispensing justice, he teaches the people "the statutes of God and His laws" (18:16).

Jethro understands the validity of the task, but counsels

Moses concerning the method he has chosen to accomplish the God-given responsibility of caring for the people. Moses is not motivated by over-ambition; he is plagued by over-conscientiousness which creates anxiety. Because of his attempt to handle this enormous task by himself, Moses is wearing himself out as well as the people (18:18). Not only is Moses overworked; his inability to hear the complaints in a timely fashion would lead to frustration and outright rebellion on the part of the people.

Most pastors have a genuine desire to care for the needs of their people or they would have sought employment in some other field. However, when a church grows beyond about 38 persons it ceases to be a single-cell church and thus one person, no matter how gifted, cannot handle all the needs of the people all the time. When someone feels that their needs are not being addressed and that no one cares for them, they often leave the church. When they leave with unresolved issues, they tell others about the neglect of their needs and create a snowball effect that does great damage to the church and its reputation in the community.

Jethro wisely suggests that Moses continue to function as the people's representative before God and, therefore, the head of the congregation. As such he will "make known the way in which they are to walk and the work they are to do" (18:20). In other words Moses is to teach them God's word so they will know how to conduct their lives and find their place of service in the community. Sounds a lot like Ephesians 4:11-12 where God instructs the pastor/teacher to equip the saints to do the work of ministry.

But there is more to Jethro's advice. Moses is to select men who will share the responsibility for leadership and care of the congregation. They must be men of integrity who fear God and hate dishonest gain (18:21). Perhaps these qualifications remind you of those in Acts 6:3 and I Timothy 3:13. These men will be placed over groups of thousands, hundreds, fifties, and tens (18:21). It is probable that the organizational plan suggested by Jethro was based on a common military model. The leaders over the smaller groups could solve most of the problems raised by their people and could bring the major issues to Moses.

Look at the practical results of this plan specified in Scripture. It would make Moses' task more reasonable since he will have others to bear the burden with him (18:22). This "shared ministry strategy" will allow him to endure (23). Is it any wonder that we are seeing pastors leaving the ministry in droves because they are burned out? Pastoral care is a challenging and demanding ministry and God never intended for it to be borne alone. Second, "all these people also will go to their place in peace" (18:23). In other words, as the needs of the individuals are met, the community experiences peace. The plan was instituted and the rest, as they say, is history.

If the church is going to provide ongoing care for every member, it must organize to do so. It is not going to happen simply because we want it to. It must be an **I**ntentional strategy that is **S**ustainable, **S**imple, and **E**xpandable. We will suggest some ideas that may help you to develop a customized strategy for your church, but first let's think through this text together.

Applying the Word

1. What prompted Jethro to worship the one true God?

2. What did he observe that caused him great concern for Moses and for the nation of Israel?

3. Why were the people gathered around Moses from morning to evening?

4. Why do you think Moses wanted to prioritize teaching the people the statues of God?

5. What did Jethro suggest that Moses do to provide the care required by the people of Israel?

6. Jethro indicates that this plan would yield two specific results. What are they?

7. What similarities do you see between this passage and Acts 6?

8. Compare it with Ephesians 4:11-16.

9. How can your small group and your church apply the principles from Jethro's advice to Moses?

Making it Stick

Our goal is to Velcro everyone in our small group and church with enough loops and hooks that they will remain active in the church and productive for the kingdom of God. We will give many suggestions that will help small groups and churches create a customized system to meet their own unique needs. Remember the key is that each small group and church must be Intentional, Sustainable, Simple, and Expandable so it can grow with you.

Personal Actions

- Pastoral care is a demanding task. Have you taken the opportunity lately to thank your pastor/staff for caring for the congregation?

- When your church designs, updates, or changes its ministry for caring for everyone, be supportive of it in spirit and attitude.

- If you are called and gifted to do so, volunteer to participate as one of the care leaders for your small group.

- Even if you aren't formally involved in the care giving ministry of your church, as part of the body of Christ, you should look regularly for the opportunity to encourage those who may be weary in their spiritual journey (1 Th. 5:14).

Small Group Actions

- Study 1 Thessalonians 5:11-15 and discuss the roles of the leaders and those of the "brethren" or church members. Do we repeat the failure of the Israelites by expecting the pastor to do the tasks assigned to the members?

- If your church plans to adopt a comprehensive organized care ministry through the small groups, ensure that your group fully understands and supports the process.

- If the church is not yet at the point of adopting a comprehensive plan, organize your group for care and ensure that each member is contacted each week.

- Organize to meet the unique and practical needs of your members.

- Pray for class members regularly and share ministry actions taken by the care ministry of your group.

Church Wide Actions

When a local church combines exciting worship with quality Bible teaching through small groups that are organized to provide ongoing care ministry to all members, they will experience Velcro community. Small groups are the most effective level for the organized care ministry because they are small enough to know the needs and large enough to organize to meet those needs. Small groups provide a natural setting for disciple-making.

Most churches already have multiple small groups that have different functions and many people may already be involved in several small groups. For example music groups, prayer groups, recreation groups, support groups, ministry teams (committees) and governing teams can fulfill a small-group assimilation role for many people. However, not everyone will be involved in such a group and many of those groups do not consider pastoral care to be part of their function. We encourage you to equip all small groups for a caring ministry. Nevertheless, each church must have a strategy that ensures that everyone will be connected to a small group that has assimilation/pastoral care as a vital part of its specific assignment.

The small-group Bible study organization provides the most comprehensive system for ensuring that everyone has a small group experience. This group also works best for the care ministry since these persons will develop affinity and love for one another as they study, pray, and fellowship together. As discussed in earlier chapters, small groups provide a wonderful entry point for non-Christian friends. Both members and non-members can be enrolled and assimilated in the same group.

Many churches have chosen to age-grade the small group Bible studies to take advantage of the power of homogeneity and receptivity. These two church health principles recognize that the gospel flows most readily through "homogenous" relationships. For example, young couples are looking to establish relationships with other couples in their stage in life. Second, age-grading provides natural movement within the small group structure and counteracts the tendency of small groups to become cliquish. If you choose not to use age-grading for organizing your small groups, you will need an organizational pattern that ensures that everyone is connected to a small group. This organizational plan must be flexible enough to allow for the creation of new units to counteract stagnancy in the small group structure and to enable the church to continue to fulfill the Great Commission.

With these few principles in mind, consider these ideas that may help you to design an organizational plan for ongoing care that meets the **ISSE** criteria. Please feel free to use any of these ideas in any manner that may seem appropriate for your church and add to them as the Spirit leads. There is no "one-size-fits-all" organizational plan for assimilation.

- An organizational plan for assimilation should be designed by those persons deemed by the leadership team to be most skilled for this task.

- The plan should be endorsed by the entire church community.

- The plan should include a commitment on the part of the church family to practice universal enrollment for all members in a small Bible study group. It is relatively simple to enroll all new-comers into a small group, but the question often arises about persons who are members of the church but not enrolled in a small group. This is a question which will only be addressed on one occasion since the church family should now commit to universal enrollment for all new members. Those who joined the church in the past but were never enrolled in a small group can be informed that the church family has decided that assimilation is a biblical mandate and has chosen to enroll everyone in a small group and that they have accordingly been enrolled in the most appropriate group. This information should be shared in a personal visit since some may offer objections to this mandatory enrollment. Objections can be lovingly and convincingly answered in a personal visit. Persons who may be offended and thus "lost" through such a process are probably only marginally involved now. If a church deems this to be too difficult a solution, members not presently enrolled in a small group could be "grandfathered." If this alternative is chosen, we do recommend that they be strongly encouraged to participate and warmly invited to the appropriate small group.

- Every effort should be made to connect people to a small group as quickly as possible when they first begin to attend the church. Most people will identify with a small group before they actually unite with the church. It is not necessary for a person to be a believer to be involved in a small group. A profession of faith should always precede actual church membership.

- If someone joins the church without having previously been connected to a small group, they can be assigned to the appropriate small group during the new-member counseling process.

- Once a new member is connected to a small group, a visit should be made by members of the small group to enhance the assimilation process. Information such as the time and place of the meeting along with information on what is presently the topic of study should be shared.

- Each small group should have adequate care ministry providers. A care leader is responsible for establishing a care group for no more than four persons or couples. If the number exceeds this goal, the task can be overwhelming. The care group exists for prayer, communication, and the discovery and meeting of needs. If we use the formula of four it would mean that a class with 24 couples on roll would need to have six care leaders. In this class there would also need to be two "care team leaders" (some churches use the deacon ministers for this task) who coordinate the work of the various care leaders, ensure that the personal needs of care leaders are being met, and who ensure accountability. You do get what you "inspect" rather than what you "expect."

- The care leader ministry must reflect the organizational

structure of the small groups. For example, many churches organize their small groups based on various departments such as young adults, median adults, etc. In this case, each department would have a "care team coordinator" who calls each class "care team leader" who, in turn, would call each care leader. This pattern is based on the Exodus 18 model we studied together. This pattern is flexible and expandable and can be used from the small one-cell church to the mega church.

- The care leader is responsible for ensuring that all four families (or persons) are called or contacted each week. The primary purpose of the call is to establish a Velcro connection by discussing small group activities, praying for needs, and discovering any needs that should be communicated to the small group. *It is critical that care leaders understand the confidential nature of their ministry. They must not share personal concerns unless given permission to do so.*

- All persons involved in the care ministry should keep careful records of calls, visits, and needs met. The care leader should know about and remember special occasions like birthdays, anniversaries, and other significant days.

- The pastor or assigned staff person should call the "care group master coordinator" early in the week. This person will call those under him/her and so the process goes down the line until every individual care group leader is called. This call is to establish ministry to those giving care and to discover what needs exist in the larger body of believers. This process will also create a climate of accountability. Once again, it is true that you get what you inspect not what you expect.

- Each small group should strive to give birth to a new small group every 12 to 18 months and to reproduce the entire small group structure. This means that the care leaders should seek to train someone in their group to be a care leader in the newly formed small group.

We are excited that you are in the process of implementing a process of outreach and inreach that will make your church a Velcro church. Don't get discouraged if it takes you a while to refine the process. The end result will be worth it in terms of intimacy of fellowship. But beyond that, it will be worth it all to see heaven populated with people who were Velcroed because you cared.

Here are a few reminders that will help your church to become a healthy Velcro church. Create an environment where your members Value every person they meet as a gift from the Lord. Engage every guest who visits your church with intentionality. Love these new friends to Christ and then Connect them to the church for their good and the good of the body. Recognize that Relationships are the key to assimilation and effective Great Commission activity. Organize for ongoing care so that your church becomes a "no-need" church like the church pictured in the book of Acts. Imagine your church doing all six of these components with consistency. The Velcro effect will help close the back door and produce dramatic results for your church if you stick to it!

Are you looking for new and refreshing resources for small group Bible study?

Auxano Press is providing a new kind of small group study that your people will be eager to study and to keep:

- small book curriculum pieces
- non-disposable
- foundation for building a Christian library
- 12- or 13-week study
- audio teacher's commentary
- free teaching helps available online
- Doctrine, Old Testament, New Testament and Bible in Life study available each year

---

SMALL BOOK CURRICULUM PIECES AVAILABLE NOW

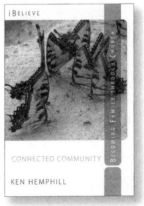

**Core Convictions:
Foundations of Faith**

**Connected Community:
Becoming Family
through Church**

For more information visit AuxanoPress.com.

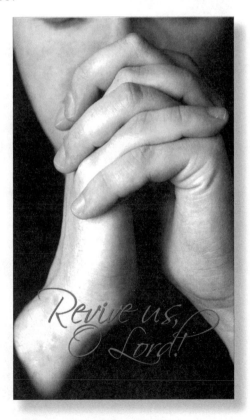

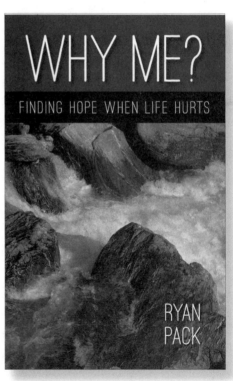